"For those who were eyewitnesses to [the] book will be a welcome reminder of [what made their] lives so special. For those who know [it,] will be an entertaining crash course o[n ...] Christian church in America for generations. For everyone, it will be a compelling testimony about the power of God to save."

Dr. Jack Graham, pastor, Prestonwood Baptist Church

"*The Jesus Revolution* has tuned my heart to a higher level of praise for a loving God who has the proven power to break through to a lost, godless, self-destructing generation and redeem it, one person at a time. If He could rescue and reset Greg Laurie—and He did—then there is no one and no generation beyond His reach. Reading this book will rekindle your prayer for revival."

Anne Graham Lotz, speaker; author, *The Daniel Prayer*; www.annegrahamlotz.org

"Back in the '60s, when I first came to Christ, you could sense a stirring out on the West Coast. God was on the move, and I was about to be swept up in the powerful flooding of the Holy Spirit that was spilling and splashing into the hearts of a million young people across America. I heard stories of how God was rescuing wayward wanderers through the Jesus Movement, sparking a revival that rocked our country and beyond. It's why Greg and Ellen's new book, *Jesus Revolution*, is so important, so needed—it documents the testimonies and events that made that period in time so unique. You, too, will be inspired and refreshed as you read the historic account of one of the most remarkable seasons of revival in the history of Christianity!"

Joni Eareckson Tada, Joni and Friends International Disability Center

"In the 1960s and '70s, God moved in a unique way, sweeping across America and transforming the lives of countless people. In their new book, *Jesus Revolution*, Pastor Greg Laurie and Ellen Vaughn take a closer look at this incredible time of evangelism and revival. This fast-paced, grace-filled, Bible-centered book will show you how God uses ordinary people to do extraordinary things."

Craig Groeschel, pastor, Life.Church; *New York Times* bestselling author

"Revival is a mile-marker that is seen throughout the centuries, with the Jesus Movement being no exception. Greg Laurie and Ellen Vaughn have given us a riveting account of a time in our nation's history where God uniquely captivated millions of hearts. This book will stir up a fresh gratitude for what God has done and a renewed hunger to see Him do even more in the years to come!"

Levi Lusko, bestselling author, *Swipe Right: The Life-and-Death Power of Sex and Romance*

"So few even realize today that many of the best things happening in our churches amount only to ripples from the 1970s revival wave called the Jesus Revolution. Greg Laurie was an eyewitness to what most have only heard about. His meaningful firsthand accounts flow through Ellen Vaughn's gripping narrative, prompting every reader to cry out 'Do it again, Lord.' Read and join those already praying to see God move afresh in such powerful ways."

Dr. James MacDonald, founder, Harvest Bible Chapel; author, *Vertical Church*

"If there was ever a time that a book like this was needed, it is now. The story of the Jesus Revolution is a compelling witness of God's power to redeem and restore human souls in the most surprising of ways, in the most chaotic of times. Brilliant work, Greg and Ellen!"

Dr. Robert Jeffress, senior pastor, First Baptist Church, Dallas, Texas; teacher, Pathway to Victory

"Stories inspire people to believe God. This is why I am so excited about this powerful book about the Jesus Revolution, because I know it will create the spiritual appetite to experience the next great move of God in our generation. There is no greater need today than for the church to be revived spiritually and for the next great spiritual awakening to occur nationally. Now is the time for the next Jesus Revolution in America!"

Dr. Ronnie Floyd, senior pastor, Cross Church; president, National Day of Prayer; past president, Southern Baptist Convention

JESUS
REVOLUTION

JESUS
REVOLUTION

HOW GOD TRANSFORMED AN
UNLIKELY GENERATION AND
HOW HE CAN DO IT AGAIN TODAY

GREG LAURIE
ELLEN VAUGHN

BakerBooks

a division of Baker Publishing Group
Grand Rapids, Michigan

© 2018 by Greg Laurie and Ellen Vaughn

Published by Baker Books
a division of Baker Publishing Group
PO Box 6287, Grand Rapids, MI 49516-6287
www.bakerbooks.com

Movie edition published 2023
ISBN 978-0-8010-9500-9

The Library of Congress has cataloged the original edition as follows:
Names: Laurie, Greg, author. | Vaughn, Ellen Santilli, author.
Title: Jesus revolution : how God transformed an unlikely generation and how he can do it again today / Greg Laurie and Ellen Vaughn.
Description: Grand Rapids : Baker Publishing Group, 2018. | Includes bibliographical references.
Identifiers: LCCN 2017061324 | ISBN 9780801075940 (cloth)
Subjects: LCSH: Jesus People—United States—History. | Revivals.
Classification: LCC BV3793 .L36 2018 | DDC 269.0973/09047—dc23
LC record available at https://lccn.loc.gov/2017061324

The authors are represented by the literary agency of Wolgemuth & Associates, Inc.

Baker Publishing Group publications use paper produced from sustainable forestry practices and post-consumer waste whenever possible.

23   24   25   26   27   28   29   7   6   5   4   3   2   1

To Greg's grandchildren, Stella, Rylie,
Lucy, Alexandra, and Christopher,
and Ellen's grandchildren, Brielle and Daniel:
may they all experience their own,
personal Jesus Revolution.

Break up your unplowed ground; for it is time to seek the LORD, until he comes and showers his righteousness on you.

Hosea 10:12

CONTENTS

Contents

PROLOGUE

Plunging In

It's 1970.

Google Earth doesn't yet exist, but imagine that it does. You are in outer space. The earth is a round blue marble. Then you zoom in, in real time, on the map of the United States, the West Coast, Southern California. You see the dark blue waters of the Pacific Ocean . . . and as you get closer, you see the long ribbon of the Pacific Coast Highway, the beach towns south of Los Angeles, the furrows of the waves. You see the slender strip of land called the Balboa Peninsula, and you draw close to Corona del Mar. There is the beach, dotted with fire pits. There is an outcropping of cliffs that form a natural amphitheater near the mouth of the harbor. The rocks look wrinkled at this height. The sun is setting.

As you get closer, you see that there is a huge crowd massing the area. At first the people look like ants. They're perched on the rocks, sitting on the sand, standing in the shallows of the rolling water. They have their arms around each other. They seem to be singing.

11

Beyond the scene on the beach, the world is a chaotic, confused place in 1970. The Vietnam War is raging. Richard Nixon is president of the United States. The nation is convulsing with divisions between young and old, black and white, and hippies and "straights," meaning conservatives. Young women are burning their bras in the streets; young men are burning their draft cards. Janis Joplin, Jimi Hendrix, and Jim Morrison rule the airwaves, though drugs will take their lives within a year. The hippie movement, born of drugs, sex, and rock and roll, has been turned inside out by disillusionment, bad trips, cynicism, and pain. For many of the flower children, their kaleidoscope colors have faded to shades of gray.

Now you are close enough to the beach to hear the music. There are simple choruses and haunting, melodic harmonies. Something about "one in the Spirit, one in the Lord." The setting looks like a baptismal scene from the New Testament except for the cutoff shorts of the slender teenaged girls. Most have long hair parted in the middle; some are shivering, sharing a striped towel, and weeping tears of joy, with huge, fresh smiles.

There is a long-haired teenaged boy. He looks like he's about seventeen. He's more quiet and reserved than the girls, as if he still carries the burdens of the past dead ends of drinking, drug use, and skeptical despair. A bearded pastor in a flowing tunic, sopping wet, dunks the young man down in the cold water for a long moment. It's as if he's been buried.

Then the hippie pastor raises the kid up, and the teenager bursts out of the sea, water streaming from his face and hair and shoulders. His heart is on his face, and he is weeping. Joy. Release. Freedom. The first thing he gasps, though, is strange:

"I'm alive!"

12

1

What Was It and Why Does It Matter?

There can't be any large-scale revolution until there's a personal revolution, on an individual level. It's got to happen inside first.

Jim Morrison

A true revival means nothing less than a revolution, casting out the spirit of worldliness and selfishness, and making God and His love triumph in the heart and life.

Andrew Murray

The hippies who plunged into the Pacific Ocean during that summer sunset in 1970 didn't know they were in a revival. They didn't even know what a revival was. They were not acquainted with Christian vocabulary words like *revival* or *salvation* or *sanctification*.

But thanks to the Beatles, Jim Morrison, and other countercultural icons of the day, the hippies did know about words like *revolution.*

They were part of a youth culture that revolted against what they called "the Establishment," the mainstream's reigning values of conformity and the rat race of material success and achievement. They were more interested in achieving higher levels of consciousness through drugs, grooving on the music of the day, and enjoying sexual adventures free from the convention of marriage. They were for the planet, flowers, and everybody just getting along.

This youth revolution was in full swing when a deeper, stronger, and more radical tide began to surge.

It was called the Jesus Revolution, or the Jesus Movement. It swelled among young people—the baby boomer generation—in the US from the late 1960s into the early 1970s. It was the largest public movement of the Holy Spirit in the United States since the celebrated revivals of the nineteenth century. National magazines wrote colorful feature stories about this mass spiritual phenomenon, as did newspapers like the *New York Times.*

More people were baptized during the Jesus Revolution than in any time since people started keeping records. They were flower children, hippies, yippies, druggies, and square church kids. Teenagers who had run away from home got saved on the streets. Junkies got clean. Churches—the ones that would accept barefoot flower children sitting on their carpets and curling their bare toes in the communion cup racks—overflowed with new believers. Bible studies caught fire in coffeehouses in Haight-Ashbury, communes in Greenwich Village, a strip joint converted into a "Christian nightclub" in San Antonio, and in public high schools, where converted hippies taught Bible studies and druggie students decided to follow Jesus, right on campus. The movement spread into dramatic charismatic renewals in various church traditions and gave birth to Jews for Jesus. Only God knows how many lives the Holy Spirit touched and transformed during that time.

In the first wave of the Jesus Revolution, the converts were mostly hippies who'd been searching for love, spiritual enlightenment, and freedom, and hadn't found it in sex, drugs, and rock and roll.

As these people—called "Jesus freaks" by other hippies—started coming into churches, there was a bit of cognitive dissonance, that psychological discomfort we all feel when we simultaneously hold two contradictory beliefs. To put it plainly, the church people knew they were *supposed* to love people different from themselves, but they found it much easier to do so in theory than in actuality.

Perhaps that's because some of the church folk had mixed cultural values with their "Christian" perspective. Being a Christian somehow had to do with conforming to cultural norms regarding hair length or conservative clothing or sturdy footwear. So while it was great to love hippies as a concept, actually doing so became a challenge for some Christians when they encountered hippies wearing beads and bells strolling barefoot down the aisles of their sanctuaries and then plopping down right next to them in their pews.

The churches that welcomed the hippies grew in grace and vigor; the ones that didn't missed both the boat and the blessing.

Soon the movement spread beyond the long-haired flower children. Soon conservative Christian kids were flashing One

Way hand signs and grooving out on the Word of God, excited about Jesus in a new way.

The Holy Spirit ignited embers of awakening and revival all over the country. Awakening: people who were spiritually dead came to know Jesus and became alive in Him. Revival: Christians who'd lost their "first love" for Christ caught a fresh wind of the Spirit, and were renewed and invigorated in their faith.

Some religious leaders, like Billy Graham and Campus Crusade founder Bill Bright, embraced the Jesus Movement. Their Explo '72 drew eighty thousand kids to the Cotton Bowl in Texas for a five-day festival of Bible study, worship, telling others about their faith, and serving needy people in the surrounding areas.

The Jesus Revolution brought new forms of worship into mainstream experience. Before it, young people in churches had two musical options: old hymns or cheery camp songs. Then, as hippie musicians who came to Jesus applied their talents to writing praise music about Him, Christian teenagers had new music to call their own. The resulting creative explosion—what's known now as contemporary Christian music—changed the face of worship in many churches for decades to come.

Many who came to faith in Christ in those heady days went on to become missionaries, pastors, and lay leaders. They had families. They started all kinds of new churches and parachurch and social justice ministries. Many of the '70s converts who became pastors started churches that grew . . . and grew. Since they'd once been outsiders, the Jesus People generation wanted to make sure their churches weren't just bastions of comfy Christians speaking a language only the faithful could understand. They welcomed outsiders, whom they called "seekers," and within a decade or two, megachurches started popping up, like very large mushrooms, across the United States.

And yes, like anything involving human beings, the Jesus Movement also had its share of flawed characters. Some were like Samson—mightily blessed by God, but then they fell off His wagon. If their paths are not always worth following, their colorful stories are still worth reading. For even when revival wanes and awakenings lull, God is still at work.

Today there's a growing sense that history has run one of its cycles, and we're back in '60s mode. At first glance, today's young people seem more tied to their iPhones and double-tall soy lattes than they are into renouncing material things, living communally, or marching in the streets like the flower children of old.

But like the hippies, millennials—people born between the early 1980s and the early 2000s—say they are hungry for authenticity, a sense of community, and real care for people who are needy and marginalized. Like the hippies, they're a bit cynical about big business, big institutions, or organized religion. Bombarded by competing content online for most of their lives, they shy away from advertising, causes, or techniques that feel superficially targeted toward them. They gravitate toward "user-generated content" that feels like it came from a real person, not a brand.

Meanwhile, their phones ping with news alerts all the time, feeding a generalized anxiety about racial unrest, environmental sustainability, gender issues, long-range missiles, terrorism, and a polarized political process full of haters. Issues like sex trafficking, genocide, starvation, and natural disasters are on their screens and in their faces all the time.

The old baby boomers were the first generation to see body bags coming back from Vietnam on the evening news, and the first actual murders on video and live TV—think the Zapruder film of the assassination of President Kennedy and the live shooting on the news, forty-eight hours later, of alleged assassin Lee Harvey Oswald.

Today's violence is constant, stark, and immediate. We see mass murders at concerts, nightclubs, offices, malls, cafes, churches, and everywhere else in real time. ISIS murders innocent victims online. Suicide bombers blow themselves up in crowds; assassins in trucks mow down pedestrians and bikers. Earthquakes, hurricanes, floods, and fires sweep through communities. People don't dance in the streets with flowers in their hair, benign and blissful. The innocence is gone. We scan crowds, alert for suspicious characters. If you see something, say something. We're all on edge. Studies show that Americans are the most stressed people on the planet. Meanwhile, wars in faraway places drone on. Afghanistan. Iraq. Iran and North Korea threaten. Russia menaces, dreaming of reclaiming its Cold War glory.

There's another harsh parallel with the '60s. After the hopeful, peaceful civil rights marches of the '60s came the assassination of Martin Luther King Jr. There were riots in the streets. Today we see ongoing, anguishing racial division. *Time* magazine called the streets of Baltimore, Ferguson, and other racially charged cities a scene from 1968. When our first African American president was elected back in 2008, polls showed that Americans were optimistic about new heights of racial unity. By the close of Mr. Obama's two terms, those cheerful expectations were gone.

On the political front, it's safe to say that we've lost the ability to have civil discourse among those who hold different points of view. The national "conversation," if you can call it that, has never been uglier, even as the many issues confronting our body politic—like ongoing debt, unemployment, health care, taxes, national security, immigration, and refugee policies—are absolutely daunting.

Spiritually, many young people are fed up with conventional church, political Christianity that is mad at everyone, and the faith-virus of affluenza, today's version of the prosperity gospel. Pew Research studies have found that the "nones"— people who self-identify as atheists or agnostics, as well as those who say their religion is "nothing in particular"—now make up almost 25 percent of US adults. (There are also a lot of Christians, young and old, who call themselves "dones," as in they are done with church, though they still like Jesus, but that's another story.)

Today, 75 percent of young people who grew up in Christian homes and churches are now abandoning their faith as young adults. More than one-third of millennials say they are unaffiliated with any faith, up 10 percentage points since 2007.

People say that they are "spiritual" but not "religious." A lot of them feel like "going to church" is irrelevant. They're impatient with big churches that are more concerned about fellowship groups than helping the poor. The seeker-friendly megachurches of their parents' generation are too slick and programmed; they want something more real, more radical, and more rugged.

As one Christian journalist summed it up,

> Millennials have a dim view of church. They are highly skeptical of religion. Yet they are still thirsty for transcendence. But when we portray God as a cosmic buddy, we lose them (they have enough friends). When we tell them that God will give them a better marriage and family, it's white noise (they're delaying marriage and kids or forgoing them altogether). When we tell them they're special, we're merely echoing what educators, coaches, and parents have told them their whole lives. But when we present a ravishing vision of a loving and holy God, it just might get their attention and capture their hearts as well.[1]

This is what we all need today, young or old. In a weary, chaotic, selfie-satiated culture, we need a big, ravishing, transcendent, and transformational vision of who God really is. That's what happened fifty years ago. It can happen again today.

This book tells the Jesus Revolution story through the experiences of one person God transformed back in the '70s, one person whose story is unique yet representative of hundreds of thousands of others. His name is Greg Laurie.

Today Greg is primarily known as a West Coast megachurch pastor and a big-arena crusade evangelist. He's one of the "usual suspects" mentioned when members of the media profile well-known pastors or Christian leaders. He's served on Billy Graham's board of directors for years. He's written lots of books; you can hear him on the radio. Perhaps he's better known on the West Coast than in other parts of the country, but many on the East Coast like him too. He's a funny, intense, creative guy. His knees never stop jiggling;

he's full of quirky, pent-up energy. He loves to eat breakfast, lunch, dinner, and anything in between. He works out. He doodles on restaurant tablecloths and has more ideas before breakfast than most of us come up with all day long. He's been studying the Bible and preaching the gospel almost all his life.

If you didn't know Greg Laurie, you might assume he was born into an affirming Christian home that was somewhat like a seminary, that he was homeschooled by a loving mother and cheered on by a godly dad who was probably a pastor himself.

Greg would be the first to say that such a scenario would have been absolutely wonderful. But he came from a far less functional home.

In 1970, Greg was just another California teenager, drifting, doing drugs, and pessimistically hating any type of authority, conformity, or convention. His dad was not a pastor; in fact, Greg did not know who his biological father was until he was well into his forties. Greg's mother was married and divorced seven times. His home of origin was a perpetual briefing on alcohol, casual sex, dysfunction, and distrust. Greg was cynical from the time he was about five years old, a skeptic who had little hope of ever having healthy relationships, let alone finding the life of love, stability, and meaning that he secretly longed for.

So it was a shock—actually, a divine surprise—when Greg Laurie came to know Jesus in 1970 and was swept right into the tide of the Jesus Movement. He didn't know that he was living in an unusual torrent of God's Spirit. He didn't know that the way he and his friends would tell people about Jesus every day—and how those people would enthusiastically come to faith in Christ—was unusual. He didn't know that being part of a church that welcomed dozens of new believers every week, and baptized thousands of new Jesus People every year, was uncommon. He thought the faith, fervor, and fruit of the Jesus Revolution was just normal Christianity. He and his friends were astonished that they got to be part of it. They were perpetually overwhelmed, in fact, that God's love story had actually included *them*.

So this is an account of some of what God did during the Jesus Revolution of the late '60s and early '70s, seen through one particular lens. As with other movements of God, we will have to wait until we get to Heaven to hear the full, enormous narrative with *all* the stories of the people God so beautifully saved and transformed during that time period, and how their lives, in turn, touched others.[2]

Our story here is more than just a vintage tale of what God did in a past generation. It's a bit of time travel, or a message in a bottle from an intriguing, long-gone era. And the message is this: *God can do it again.* He can surprise us all with a new season of extraordinary, radical, spine-tingling hope, and a new flood of His Holy Spirit on a new generation.

A new Jesus Movement would not look the same as it did fifty years ago. But in our own unruly times, God can certainly bring powerful revival to His church and an awakening among people who don't yet know Him.

But that is something He tends to do only if people admit they need Him.

The hippies, flower children, and others who came to Jesus back in the '60s were *desperate*. They were willing to go to any lengths, or on any trip, to find what they were looking for. They'd throw off their clothes or their conventions, longing to break free of sin and shame. And when they heard the gospel—the good news about Jesus Christ, and that He was real and alive and loved the whole world—it blew their minds, to put it in '60s vernacular. Their desperate search was satisfied.

So that's the central question for all of us today. Young or old, are we going through the motions, comfortable and complacent, consuming some brand of cultural churchianity that has little to do with the electrifying gospel of Jesus Christ? Are we really desperate to know God, to embrace the fresh, mysterious, powerful wind of His Holy Spirit?

Revival, after all, is not about human plans, programs, campaigns, or particular denominational movements. It comes from the real revolution that only God can bring.

That word, *revolution*, cuts both ways. It's a paradox.

First, revolution means a sudden, radical, complete change in a structure in favor of a new system.

Think about it in a personal sense. The spiritual revolution means that Jesus touches our lives and radically transforms them from the inside out.

The old allegiances are gone, the old structures torn down and replaced by the fresh presence of His Spirit and the new paths of obedience. Even if we don't happen to have a dramatic experience, when we're saved by grace, the reality in terms of our eternal standing is that it's a new beginning. The past is finished and gone, the new has come. We belong to Jesus and will see Him in Heaven when we die. Boom.

But the revolution that Jesus brings is more than just this sudden, radical new beginning. Revolution also means the act of revolving in a circle, back to a fixed point. It's like the rolling of a wheel, revolving, returning to the same place, yet moving forward. So the Jesus Revolution, really, is not just a one-time, dramatic upheaval. It is also the process of an ongoing relationship with God. A long obedience in the same direction.

In that continuing journey, we can grow cold, distant, and apathetic. We can lose the fire. Whether you're a pastor or a person on the street, that's the challenge. We all know so many, whether celebrated religious leaders or our friends or ourselves, who've lost that first love of Christ and drifted away.

How do we keep it fresh?

Churches across the country, both large and small, are holding prayer sessions, yearning for revival, with people on their knees crying out, "Oh Lord, please do it again!" Evangelistic, revival-oriented movements are introducing young people today to the Jesus Movement of the late '60s, hosting all-day seminars about what God did then and how revival might come again. Contemporary magazines are posting articles with titles like "What We Can Learn from the Jesus Movement." Christian colleges and universities are bringing in guest professors to teach on the worship music of the Jesus People. Millennials are organizing big conferences that focus on mass awakenings and revivals, seeking a new Jesus Revolution for the twenty-first century.

Again, this isn't just a peace-sign nostalgia fest for old baby boomers. Telling stories of former revivals can help spark repentant and expectant hearts in all who long for a new Jesus Revolution today. As Isaiah 64:5 says, God meets with those who remember His ways.

Maybe some will read this book, at first, for the exotic stories from the '60s. Hopefully those stories will awaken or affirm a desperate desire in people who are hungry for the same sort of movement of God's Spirit. That's great. But this book is also about the ongoing revolution over the long run, how the wheel of faith turns in all our lives, and the surprising ways in which God can make it new and fresh. So if you come for the history, stay for the more important story of the personal revolution that God can do in you. Today.

2

A Black-and-White Decade

The pace of the fifties seemed slower, almost languid. Social ferment, however, was beginning just beneath this placid surface.

David Halberstam, *The Fifties*

They danced down the streets like dingledodies, and I shambled after as I've been doing all my life after people who interest me, because the only people for me are the mad ones, the ones who are mad to live, mad to talk, mad to be saved, desirous of everything at the same time, the ones that never yawn or say a commonplace thing, but burn, burn, burn like fabulous yellow roman candles exploding like spiders across the stars and in the middle you see the blue centerlight pop and everybody goes "Awww!"

Jack Kerouac, *On the Road*

To understand the free-for-all of the late 1960s, you have to start in the boxy 1950s. It's a decade that even baby boomers like Greg Laurie know little about, really, even though we lived in it. But the '50s set the stage to shape the world for all of us today; it's important to know the history.

It's complicated. But if you were white and middle class in America, the time period between 1950 and 1960 is often presented as that cheerful decade in which the American family and other institutions provided normalcy after the turmoil of World War II. Americans had come through the hard times of the Great Depression of the 1930s and the horrors of the war years. Now there was a sense of a new wind blowing: American prosperity. Many a man of the Greatest Generation finished college on the GI Bill and went to work in his conservative gray flannel suit, making an average of $4,100 a year. At 5:01 p.m. he'd return to his tidy suburban home, which cost him $22,000, situated on a block full of zippy kids riding bikes with no helmets and dogs running free with no leashes.

Our crew-cut man was met at the front door by his lovely wife, who was likely wearing pearls, a dress, and an apron. She did not work outside the home.[1] Wifey had a hot dinner in the oven, courtesy of her new Mixmaster and her electric stove. After meat loaf, mashed potatoes with gravy, green-bean casserole, and strawberry Jell-O, everyone would gather around the rabbit-eared black-and-white TV. It did not have a big screen, but it weighed a ton and took about a week to warm up. The fam would eagerly watch shows like *Leave It to Beaver*, *Father Knows Best*, or *The Adventures of Ozzie and Harriet*, which were short on adventure but long on wholesome life lessons. Then everyone would put on their striped pajamas with piping on the lapels, drink a glass of whole milk, and jump into bed. The TV itself went to bed at midnight, signing off with the national anthem playing to scenes of saluting soldiers and a waving American flag. Then the screen went to a rainbow test pattern until it woke up the following morning.

Television's effect on mainstream baby boomers' experience was huge. Social critics say that TV homogenized America, just like a big carton of frothy, white milk from cows on steroids. For the first time, persuasive images and cultural "norms" were right there for all to consume, in your own living room, regardless of where you lived. While books, newspapers, and radio targeted regionally or educationally diverse audiences, television story lines and advertisers catered to the lowest common denominator in an effort to target everyone. People in California, Iowa, and the East Coast all saw the same shows and the same advertisements. Television had a nationalizing influence, creating or revealing realities that trumped local, traditional ties to neighborhoods, churches, or ethnic groups.[2]

In this, television has been called a great equalizer, though it was very selective about who it equalized. In TV Land—with a few rare exceptions—everyone was white.

And on 1950s TV, sex didn't exist. *I Love Lucy*'s Lucille Ball and Desi Arnaz, married in real life, went to bed on-screen in cute little twin beds separated by a chaste nightstand. It was a mystery how little Ricky was ever conceived. Another mainstream message was that it was normal, healthy, and desirable to smoke cigarettes. For example, NBC's nightly news broadcast peddled Camels relentlessly; everyone knew that Hollywood stars and anyone else who was cool smoked like chimneys all day long.

Life wasn't all cheerful TV and status quo family life in the suburbs, of course. There were cranky rebels like Jack

Kerouac, whose drug- and alcohol-induced rants on life in America emerged from the frenzied pages of *On the Road*, the countercultural classic of the day. Kerouac and other Beat writers, along with abstract expressionists like Jackson Pollock, questioned mainstream culture's prevailing values. Other, lesser-known kindred spirits wore goatees and jaunty French berets, played bongo drums, smoked weed, and hung out in Greenwich Village and other cultural scenes that didn't care for the 1950s' conformity, consumerism, and predictability.

Meanwhile, in spite of the great victories of World War II, the world was still a scary place. The worldwide conflict was soon followed by the Korean War of the early 1950s, which killed 37,000 Americans and ended with a demilitarized zone separating communist North Korea from democratic South Korea. A peace agreement was never actually signed; the dark and volatile tensions endure to this day.

In 1949, the Soviet dictator Joseph Stalin detonated the first Soviet atomic bomb. The race was on to develop a more deadly hydrogen bomb, which the US did in 1952. Tested on a remote atoll in the Pacific Ocean, it created a cloud 100 miles wide and 25 miles high, killing all life on the surrounding islands.

The Soviets surprised the world by detonating their own hydrogen bomb in 1953, and then a bigger, badder one in 1955. Such deadly weapons demanded delivery systems with far more range than conventional airplanes. In 1957, the Soviet Union launched Sputnik, the first satellite to orbit the earth; the message was clear that they now could attack anywhere, at any time. The US launched its own first satellite in 1958.

The Space Race and the Cold War were on. By the end of the 1950s, both the US and the Soviet Union had enough nuclear buildup so even if one side launched an annihilating attack, the other side could retaliate with a similar, obliterating response. The resulting term is still familiar today: mutually assured destruction.

This grim competition trickled down to everyday experience. Any old geezer who was in elementary school in the 1950s can tell you about "bomb drills," a routine part of school life. These "duck and cover" exercises were designed by the Federal Civil Defense Administration for "emotion management." In the middle of the school day, a siren would howl and small children, all managing their emotions properly, would dive beneath their little wooden desks, which they were told would protect them in case of nuclear attack.

Right.

The fear of the end of the world at the hand of godless communists was exacerbated by witch hunts at home. Senator Joseph McCarthy embarked on a mission to flush commies from the government and woodwork of American life. His Committee on Un-American Activities reflected an atmosphere of overt threats in the world at large; it fomented hidden fears right here at home. FBI director J. Edgar Hoover maintained secret files on everyone from Dr. Martin Luther King Jr. to the political stars of the Kennedy family to journalists and suspicious Hollywood celebrities. Potential blackmail, fear, and intimidation were political weapons.

The biggest blight on the "innocent" 1950s, however, was the status of race relations in America. The injustices are too many to recount. The Civil War had been fought less than a century earlier; it's shocking to realize that racial segregation was the law of the land in America, with deep-seated bigotry the attitude of many. Interracial marriage was illegal, underscoring yet again that the notion that African Americans were "separate but equal" was only halfway true.

While legal segregation of schools was abolished by the Supreme Court in 1954, all public segregation would not be banned until 1964. African Americans were known as Negroes, colored people, or other derogatory terms. They were forced to use separate bathrooms, telephone booths, seats on buses, and entrances to movie theaters. An eloquent southern preacher named Dr. Martin Luther King became more and more well known, stirring the hopes of millions with his vision of nonviolent resistance and racial equality. Black churches provided the scriptural language that undergirded the movement. In 1955 a gutsy and faith-filled black woman named Rosa Parks refused to move to the back of a city bus in Montgomery, Alabama, when a white man "needed" her seat. Parks's civil disobedience set a trail that would blaze for many more in the 1960s and onward. But in the '50s any fruit of the civil rights movement was still a dream, and much blood would be shed for decades to come.

Back in suburbia, mainstream American pop culture hummed right along. War hero Dwight Eisenhower, a smiling grandpa, was shown on TV playing with his grandchildren in the White House. People drove giant cars with cool, colorful fins, enjoying more disposable income than previous decades, and ate fifteen-cent hamburgers at a new restaurant called McDonald's. Elvis was still in the building; in fact, he'd just released his first hit, "Heartbreak Hotel." Glamorous stars like Marilyn Monroe, Clark Gable, John Wayne, Rita

Hayworth, and Gary Cooper filled the big screen. You could watch them at a drive-in movie theater for twenty-five cents.

God was popular too. In 1957, the Treasury Department started issuing bills emblazoned with the motto "In God We Trust." Nationwide church membership grew at a faster rate than the general population.[3] When CBS News recently conducted a poll asking people to choose a decade to which they'd like to time travel, the nostalgic majority chose the 1950s—a time when marriages, children, churches, and families all boomed.

If these institutions were the cherished norms of the decade, Greg Laurie, born in 1952, didn't experience any of them. Unlike the TV shows that glorified America's ideal childhood, his mom was no June Cleaver, and his father didn't know best.

Greg never knew his father, and his restless mother, Charlene, looked a lot more like Marilyn Monroe than Mrs. Cleaver. She'd run away from her strict, fundamentalist Christian home when she was seventeen, seeking the bright lights of Hollywood. She didn't hit the big time, but in small-time bars she was a star. Men found her irresistible, like the sailor with strawberry-blond hair she met on the dance floor one night in 1952 in Long Beach, California. Maybe it was a one-night stand; maybe it lasted a week or two. But the sailor was soon gone, and when Charlene discovered she was pregnant, she quickly married a guy named Kim.

Greg was born in December of 1952. As a little boy, he thought Kim was his father. It never made sense to him as to why his "dad," often drunk, would rage at him, beat him, ignore him, or prefer his two older brothers. It wasn't until Greg was about forty that he discovered Kim was not his biological father, his "brothers" were not actually bros, and his paternity was a lie.

In between husbands, Charlene and Greg moved around a lot. They lived in motels. Greg was a creative, observant kid, artistically gifted and pretty good at figuring out if adults were sincere or not. In the evenings, Charlene would hang out in clubs while Greg ate a hamburger and drew cartoons. Since he was in elementary school, he wasn't technically allowed to sit at the bar, but most bartenders liked the little blond artist and bent the rules for him.

The classic *Star Wars* movies hadn't been made yet—they were still in a future galaxy far, far away—but many of Greg's childhood memories feature characters who seemed a lot like aliens from the famous *Star Wars* bar scene. There was Fuzzy, an adult who was even shorter than Greg. Fuzzy had no hair. He had strong opinions. After a few rounds, he'd usually hold forth to Greg about the proper way to make a tuna fish sandwich. No pickles. The bar was dimly illuminated by shellacked puffer fish whose insides had been scooped out and replaced with lightbulbs. Fishnets hung from the ceiling. An ancient diving helmet sat on the bar like a decapitated human head.

At the end of long evenings at the bar, Charlene wasn't always steady on her feet. Sometimes there would be a man to help her walk straight, and they'd all head home, wherever home was that month.

Sometimes, when he became inconvenient to Charlene, Greg would live with his grandparents. Mama Stella and Daddy Charles went to church a lot and had a lot of strict rules, which is why their daughter Charlene had run away. But Greg loved his grandparents. As a child, his only exposure to religion was through them. They had a portrait of a pale Jesus on their living room wall. His long, blondish hair was parted in the middle, and he didn't make eye contact. He was just looking up, up, and away, to some distant place like Heaven.

Greg's grandparents loved Billy Graham crusades. Unlike that pale Jesus, Billy Graham, through the magic of television, looked right at people when he preached. At the time he was a celebrity, almost like a movie star. He was young and handsome and a friend of the president. Greg thought he was pretty cool, particularly at the end of the crusades. He'd always say, "Just write to me, Billy Graham, Minneapolis, Minnesota. That's all the address you need."

Who else in the world could you write to with just his name and his town on the envelope? Greg thought. *He's like Santa Claus, care of the North Pole!*

What kids like Greg did not realize at the time was that Billy Graham would become the primary religious figure in America for the next six decades. He would be one of the ten most admired men in the US every year for sixty years.

His evangelistic crusades—stadium meetings with singers, testimonies, and Graham's energized preaching—had been immensely successful in Los Angeles, Boston, Washington, London, and New York. His *Hour of Decision* radio program was hugely popular. He was written up all the time in *Christianity Today*, the new magazine he helped found in 1957. He was the standard-bearer for the evangelical movement in America at that time.

And though Graham was the darling of white churchianity, he did not ignore the situation of black Americans. He reached out to Dr. Martin Luther King and other African American pastors. In 1957 he invited Dr. King to New York to discuss the racial situation with him and his colleagues, and to lead Graham's enormous Madison Square Garden crusade in prayer. Not too many white evangelical preachers were doing that back then.

Graham had critics on all sides. Some didn't support his racial reconciliation stance. Some felt he didn't go far enough and should have done so much more for the civil rights movement. Some didn't care for his friendships with the rich and powerful. But for the most part, both Christians and non-Christians *liked* Billy Graham. They respected the courage of his convictions, his trademark but natural way of preaching the Bible plainly all over the world, and the way he steadily conducted himself with refreshing moral integrity over the course of his long ministry.

Greg Laurie didn't know back then that Billy Graham would eventually become his mentor and friend. Nothing really penetrated his mind or heart from Graham's televised crusades. And Greg knew nothing of the classic 1950s life at the wholesome suburban house with the picket fence. But he did know a lot about cleaning up his mom after she'd passed out again. He knew a lot about fending for himself. And somehow—maybe because of the pixie-dust veneer of that cheerful decade, or perhaps from watching a few too many episodes of *Lassie*—Greg believed that one day life would be much, much better.

3

The Wonderful World of Color

At the beginning of a decade when everything was beginning to seem possible, nothing seemed impossible.

Margot Lee Shetterly, *Hidden Figures*

The people who invented the twenty-first century were pot-smoking, sandal-wearing hippies from the West Coast like Steve, because they saw differently. . . . The sixties produced an anarchic mind-set that is great for imagining a world not yet in existence.

Bono, as quoted in Walter Isaacson, *Steve Jobs*

A lot of people today speak almost nostalgically about the 1960s. They rave about vinyl records, great music, and groovy fashions. Yes. But to understand the forces that birthed the cultural revolution and shaped the funky characters of the Jesus Movement—like Greg Laurie—we need to take a deeper magical mystery tour of the time period.

They say that if you remember the '60s, then you weren't there. But maybe that's not true. It was a season that was both mellow and radical; its pilgrims experienced a sensual explosion in which it seemed everything was sharper, clearer, richer, and deeper.

Most people remember the sights of it all: the colors. A decade that started in black and white, as dull and conservative as a military crew cut, bloomed into a bodacious bounty of flower-power pop art, neon peace signs, skies full of diamonds, and visions through kaleidoscope eyes.

And the smells. There was that burnt-green smell of marijuana, and the sweat of hundreds of thousands of your closest friends at Woodstock and the other concerts and love-ins of the era. The scent of sea salt, surf, and Coppertone at the beach. The aromas of hot coffee, or jugs of cheap red wine, at poetry readings and love-ins and urban coffeehouses.

Taste. If the mainstream trends of the '60s followed the new fast-food giant, McDonald's, and the conveniences of mass-produced frozen dinners with their uniform rectangles of robot food, the hippies were trying to get back to the garden, anticipating the organic and slow-food trends of our own day. "Welcome to Our Space. Positive energy projection is the trip," proclaimed a menu at a hippie café in northern California. "Care in the preparation of food requires time, especially if we're busy! So please take a deep breath, relax and dig on the love & artistry about you. May all our offerings please you. Peace within you."

Touch. Besides drugs—and helped along by drugs—the biggest upheaval of the decade was the sexual revolution. Rejecting the double standards or cloistered sexuality of the 1950s, the young people of the '60s happily rode a tide of free love, sexual experimentation, and the beginnings of the women's movement, all helped along by the introduction of the birth control pill into the US market in 1961.

Sometimes the senses all seemed to merge, like on those LSD trips when people thought they could smell colors or taste music. Or sometimes senses all went away, as for those who sought higher consciousness through Eastern religions and emptied themselves of everything.

The one thing everyone agrees on, however, is the power of the *sounds* of the '60s. Even today's twentysomethings who know nothing about the decade talk nostalgically about those days of the best music of all time: the Beatles, the Rolling Stones, the Doors, the Who, Jimi Hendrix, Pink Floyd, the Kinks, Creedence Clearwater Revival, Cream, the Beach Boys, the Byrds, the Grateful Dead, Bob Dylan . . . the list, like the beat, goes on. And on.

Much of the music mirrored what was happening in popular culture, even as it led the way. Back then, if you listened to what the Beatles were doing, you pretty much had a bead on youth culture. "I want to hold your hand" became "Why don't we do it in the road?" "Love, love me, do" became "I'd love to turn you on." If George Harrison was into Eastern religion and the Maharishi and sitars, next thing you knew, everyone was singing about Vishnu and checking out transcendental meditation. If John Lennon said the Beatles were more popular than Jesus—in spite of the uproar from angry pastors with crew cuts—most people under thirty just shrugged and agreed with John.

Beatles aside, here's a black-and-white scene from the very beginning of the decade, one that changed the stage for the wonderful world of color.

September 26, 1960

The setting is a bland television studio in Chicago. The camera is focused on two men in business suits. One man is sweating, mopping his face, his dark eyes darting back and forth; he is pale, thin, and looks exhausted. The other is tanned, rested, and confident, looking straight into the camera, right into the eyes of America. Even the black-and-white TVs of the day tell the story: Senator John F. Kennedy, facing off against Vice President Richard Nixon, is the golden man of the moment.

Nixon had been in the hospital, lost twenty pounds, and was sick that evening of the first televised presidential debate. He'd refused television makeup, and his heavy five o'clock shadow made his face look shady. He looked so bad that his mother called him after the broadcast to see if he was all right.

Content-wise, each candidate made his points; in fact, most radio listeners thought that Nixon had won the debate. But television viewers had the opposite reaction. Sweaty Nixon looked like a jowly mutt, and to millions of newly minted American television watchers, there was no contest. Who would want to vote for a clammy crank? Give us the debonair, handsome one with the amazing hair!

Though charisma had always had its part in the political process, television's magnified lens meant that forever onward, until Jesus returns, political discourse would now be shaped by image over substance.

Still, the handsome, young Senator Kennedy prevailed in the 1960 election by only a narrow margin. And yes, Richard Nixon came back in 1968 and created his own unique presidential history in the '70s. But in January 1961, President Kennedy and his sophisticated wife, Jackie, swept into the White House on a glamorous tide of youth, charm, art, and culture.

A month before John Kennedy's inauguration, a coalition of communists and insurgents called the Vietcong had organized to fight against the existing regime in South Vietnam. In early 1961, President Kennedy sent an evaluation team to Vietnam; they recommended a buildup of American military, economic, and technical aid to confront this communist threat. Concerned about a domino effect in Southeast Asia, with countries tumbling to communist rule one by one, the Kennedy White House quietly increased the US presence in Vietnam.

Then Nikita Khrushchev, leader of the Soviet Union, put the youthful President Kennedy to the test. (Khrushchev, famously belligerent, had lost his temper at a United Nations General Assembly session in 1960, ripped off his shoe, and started beating his desk with it.) The USSR had long wanted beachheads for nuclear weapons able to strike the United States, and on October 14, 1962, an American spy plane photographed a Soviet medium-range ballistic missile being assembled for installation on the island of Cuba. This was ninety miles from the coast of Florida; a launch on the US from Cuba would mean the death of eighty million Americans within ten minutes.

The Cuban Missile Crisis brought America to the actual brink of nuclear war with the Soviet Union. It seemed that the world as we knew it would end in a mushroom cloud; it seemed all those bomb drills would come, in fact, to a horrific reality. There seemed no way out until, thirteen days later, the standoff between the communist leader and the young

American president ended. The USSR agreed to remove its missiles if America agreed not to attack Cuba.

It was a reprieve, but no one knew for how long. There was little cause to feel confident about lasting peace in a Cold War world.

The following summer, the two superpowers did sign a treaty limiting nuclear testing and installed a state-of-the-art instant communications system in the White House and the Kremlin. Even youngsters knew about the "hotline" that would protect the world from nuclear war: it looked like a toddler's toy, a bulky red rotary phone that would allow the superpowers to talk each other down the tree of mutually assured destruction. (Actually, messages between Kennedy and Khrushchev would be encrypted and take minutes to reach the other leader. It was considered revolutionary in 1963, a great improvement over the regular transatlantic phone call from the White House, which had to be bounced between several countries before it reached the Kremlin and was consequently just a teeny bit prone to interception.)

As President Kennedy told Americans in a sober speech in June 1963, the hoped-for cooperation between the superpowers recognized our mutual humanity. "In the final analysis," he said poignantly, "our most basic common link is that we all inhabit this small planet. We all breathe the same air. We all cherish our children's future. And we are all mortal."

Five months later, President Kennedy's own mortal run on this small planet ended. Ask any baby boomer, and they can tell you in a heartbeat where they were on November 22, 1963.

The images are seared in our minds. The motorcade of open-topped black limousines in Dallas, Texas. The waving crowds, craning to get a view of JFK and Jackie, so elegant in her famous pink Chanel suit and her matching pillbox hat. She carried a bouquet of blood-red roses as she and the president waved to the adoring crowds.

Texas governor John Connally and his wife, Nellie, rode in the limo seat in front of the president and first lady. Nellie turned around. "Mr. President," she called above the crowd noise, smiling big like the Texan she was, "you can't say Dallas doesn't love you!"

A few seconds later there was a rifle shot. Then another. The president and Governor Connally were both hit, though not mortally. Then came the third shot, the one that took off the top of the president's skull and blew part of his bone and brain matter onto the back of the limousine. There was Jackie Kennedy, crawling in that moment of horror onto the trunk to retrieve it; a Secret Service agent threw himself into the car and it screeched toward the hospital as Jackie cradled her ruined husband in her arms.

Then the aftermath, the images that flooded national television.

The president of the United States, declared dead on national television by a stunned and grief-stricken Walter Cronkite. Shock. Disbelief. America came to a halt. The president's seat in the limousine: red roses and blood. A new image: a dazed Jackie Kennedy, the pink Chanel suit smeared with gore, standing by Vice President Lyndon Johnson and his wife on Air Force One as Johnson is sworn in as the new president. JFK's coffin is in the back of the plane.

Two days later, millions watched NBC's live coverage of events as JFK's accused assassin, a malcontent named Lee Harvey Oswald, was being transferred from the Dallas Police Headquarters to jail. Handcuffed to a local detective,

Oswald was surrounded by law enforcement as he was escorted through the basement of the building.

At 11:21 a.m. local time, Jack Ruby, a Dallas strip club operator with ties to the Mafia, suddenly lunged out of the crowd, stuck a handgun within inches of Oswald's gut, and pulled the trigger. An ambulance rushed Oswald to Parkland Memorial Hospital—the same emergency room where frenzied doctors had fought to save President Kennedy from his mortal wound two days earlier. Oswald died at 1:07 p.m.

If life as usual had already felt fragile, now all bets were off. The vital, powerful, golden president had been killed by a no-name, dishonorably discharged, communist loser. Then the assassin himself was assassinated—right in front of everyone in the nation, on live television. Now anything could happen in America.

——————

During the grim months after President Kennedy's assassination and the tough challenges of Lyndon Johnson's new presidency, there were still diversions.

Perhaps the biggest national distraction was the arrival in February 1964 of that original boy band from Britain, whose latest song had just hit number one on the US charts. Teenaged girls screamed and fainted when the group arrived in New York surrounded by reporters. Parents across the country wondered what all the fuss was about. All Mom and Dad knew was that the band was named after insects. Beatles.

Seventy-three million fellow Americans, including eleven-year-old Greg Laurie, camped out in front of their big-box TVs when the Beatles sang live on the *Ed Sullivan Show*.

Strangers to the times need to understand that the *Ed Sullivan Show* was a huge deal, a "really big shew," as he used to say back in the day. Sullivan hosted the longest-running variety show in the history of American television. In an era before there were a million TV channels and a billion other entertainment options, he ruled the airwaves. Families across America gathered around the TV on Sunday nights at 8:00 p.m. It was a national ritual.

Since Sullivan had almost no personality of his own, he had a unique ability to highlight his guests' personalities. He hunched his shoulders and mumbled, seeming to have a speech impediment or at least unusual syntax. *Time* magazine said that "his smile is that of a man sucking a lemon . . . yet, instead of frightening children, Ed Sullivan charms the whole family."[1]

Sixty percent of the televisions in America were tuned in to watch the Beatles on Ed's show.

The Fab Four sang a few of their greatest hits like "She Loves You" and "I Want to Hold Your Hand." John, Paul, George, and Ringo wore black suits with skinny ties and gently shook their mop-tops while they sang. They were in their early twenties at the time; Ed kept beaming and calling them "talented youngsters."

The British Invasion had begun.

There was another invasion, of course, one far more significant than the trends of pop culture, though it merged with them to create the consciousness of a generation. America's involvement in Southeast Asia had begun with a cadre of political and military advisors, like a trickle of stones sliding down a hill. But those stones became an avalanche, and eventually tens of thousands of young Americans found themselves sliding into the jungles of Vietnam, not quite knowing what they were fighting for.

In early 1965, the US commenced Operation Rolling Thunder, a gradual and sustained bombing of North Vietnam. It was designed to boost morale in the non-communist South and to destroy the North's transportation system, industrial base, and air defenses, as well as disrupt the steady flow of fighters and weapons into the South. Rolling Thunder would roll for the next three and a half years as the storm in Vietnam got stronger and the voices crying out against it at home got louder.

On March 16, an eighty-two-year-old Detroit pacifist named Alice Herz set herself on fire to protest the war in Vietnam. She died the next day.

Elsewhere, young men started publicly burning their draft cards. Students for a Democratic Society, or SDS, organized opposition to the war, and protests began to simmer and explode on college campuses across the country.

By April 1965, twenty-five thousand American soldiers were patrolling the rice paddies of Vietnam. By the end of the year that number would be two hundred thousand.

A lot of young Americans—both in Southeast Asia, where drugs were plentiful and cheap, and at home—were embracing the growing drug culture as the gateway to spiritual enlightenment, good times, or just an escape from the status quo. Marijuana was everywhere, but LSD was the drug movement's poster child. It stimulated serotonin receptors in the brain; you never knew just where you would go or how you would feel, but you could drop a tab and take an eight-hour trip without ever leaving your chair. It was legal in the US until the mid-1960s.

The Pied Pipers of the day, the Beatles, first got into LSD in the spring of 1965. John Lennon and George Harrison were at a party in England with their wives, and their obliging host dropped sugar cubes laced with LSD into their after-dinner coffee.

"I had such an overwhelming feeling of well-being, that there was a God, and I could see him in every blade of grass. It was like gaining hundreds of years of experience in 12 hours," George later told *Rolling Stone.* After they got back home, John said, "God, it was just terrifying, but it was fantastic. George's house seemed to be just like a big submarine."[2]

Paul McCartney waited a year or so to drop acid. He said it opened his eyes to "the fact that there is a God. . . . It is obvious that God isn't in a pill, but it explained the mystery of life." Then the drug "started to find its way into everything we did, really. It colored perceptions. I think we started to realize that there weren't as many frontiers as we'd thought there were. And we realized we could break barriers."[3]

By halfway through the decade of the 1960s, there were two distinct Americas.

One was the conventional, achievement-driven, work-ethic world that had followed the '50s, populated mostly by people over the age of thirty. The other was a growing youth counterculture that rejected mainstream values of conformity, convention, and climbing the corporate ladder. The new culture embraced the planet, higher consciousness, and alternative realities. Drugs were a way to enlightenment, life was about making love not war, possessions ended up possessing you, music was truth, and freedom was the ultimate high.

By mid-1965, this hip youth movement had been tagged with its own noun, and the word *hippie* found its way into news reports. Fathers who knew best cautioned their kids from turning into dreaded hippies with long hair and bad values.

One of those dads was a conservative, unremarkable California pastor named Charles Ward Smith.

And no one could have guessed, at the time, that God would use Chuck Smith as a wild, culture-changing revolutionary.

4

The Pastor
Who Downscaled

It is a safe thing to trust Him to fulfill the desires which
He creates.

Amy Carmichael

Chuck Smith was thirty-eight in the mid-1960s. That made
him old. He was a comfortable-looking, unremarkable guy
with a big smile and bushy eyebrows. Back when he was in
high school in Southern California he'd been a promising
athlete and an excellent student; he was offered a full football scholarship to the Naval Academy. He'd thought about
going to medical school. He was gifted with his hands; he
knew how to fix things.

But though he had promising paths open to him, Chuck
Smith was a man who wanted, foremost, to do what he believed God was calling him to do. He'd grown up listening
to his mother read the Bible; he sensed that God wanted

him to be a pastor. So he went to a small Bible college and learned the Scriptures forward and backward. He might not accomplish great things in a worldly sense, he thought, but he just wanted God to use him.

Little did Chuck Smith know God would in fact use him in a small cultural explosion called the Jesus Revolution.

Early on, Chuck had found that being a pastor was frustrating. There were years of slow growth, if any, in the little Foursquare Bible churches he led in Corona, California. His denomination wanted him to be successful. Chuck wanted to be successful. For a dynamic superachiever, it was hard. Regardless of all the well-constructed sermons he preached and all the zippy contests and membership drives he started, his churches just weren't growing.

Then one day, while he was preaching, Chuck looked out over his congregation . . . and he suddenly realized he knew everybody sitting in the pews. And there was not one single unbelieving person there. It hit him: the church wasn't growing because no one in the congregation was bringing friends or neighbors or coworkers or random acquaintances with them on Sundays. They were all just talking to themselves, over and over.

Chuck switched from preaching on random, catchy topics to teaching through big sections of the Bible, pouring the Word of God from the pulpit. He started in the Gospel of John, unfolding the Jesus story as John had laid it out in the first century. He and his wife, Kay, started holding Bible studies in their home. Dozens of people showed up, hungry to hear the Bible laid out in clear, applicable ways.

The Bible study people flooded the church. Chuck's congregation soon doubled in size.

Chuck had heard somewhere that preaching through the book of Romans would transform any church. So he began to preach verse by verse on Romans, the apostle Paul's great declaration of the gospel. The first thing Chuck discovered was that the book of Romans transformed *him*.

"I really discovered grace," he said later. "I had been trying to serve God by works. I had been trying so hard to do everything right and obligate God to bless me. But of course you can't earn blessings. Then I began to recognize the goodness and blessings of what God has already done."

God's grace changed Chuck Smith . . . and it changed his church. People were excited enough about the gospel to actually invite their friends to come to church to hear it.

Then, while the church in Corona was growing and the future looked bright, Chuck Smith sensed God calling him to do something that was as counterintuitive as his earlier decision to go into the pastorate rather than become a doctor or a football star. A dwindling little church called Calvary Chapel in Costa Mesa, California, invited Chuck to come on board. When Chuck told Kay that he was actually considering this downscale move, she thought he was joking.

But God was up to something.

Chuck, Kay, and their four kids moved to Costa Mesa in December 1965. The church had peeling paint, squeaky floors, and a less-than-professional mural painted on the side wall of the dingy baptistery. Its thirty members had pretty low expectations. But over the months, Chuck carefully made some changes in those expectations.[1]

He brought order to charismatic expressions in public meetings. The church had a few individuals who tended to burst forth in unintelligible, uninterpreted utterances on

Sunday mornings, which would have confused visitors, except any visitors had already been scared away. Chuck laid out guidelines that would limit such things to that which was understandable and in order. He changed the church's habit of begging and lecturing regarding members' giving practices. He created a more welcoming atmosphere in terms of plain old handshaking friendliness. He created a robust appreciation of the great hymns of the faith and the importance of music in worship.

But most centrally, Chuck focused on preaching the Word of God clearly and passionately. Week by week, as he exposited its clear and whole gospel of grace, the church started to grow. As they had done in Corona, Chuck and Kay hosted Bible studies in their home. Within eighteen months, the church had quadrupled in size. The overflowing building had been painted, cleaned, and spruced up, reflecting the new energy in the congregation.

Still, the growing church was pretty homogenous. There were nice ladies wearing pastel dresses with matching pocketbooks and nylons with sensible, low-heeled pumps, businessmen outfitted in black suits and narrow ties, and small, clean children in their Sunday best. The gathering looked pretty much like churches in suburban America had always looked: a reflection of the prevailing values of the still-conservative culture around it.

To speak generally, maybe the good people in many American churches at the time were a bit like the people Jesus Christ encountered in His own place of worship about two thousand years earlier.

Soon after Jesus started His public ministry in Israel, He went back to his hometown, Nazareth. On the Jewish Sabbath day, He went into the synagogue, just like He always did when He was home. Jesus looked like a hippie—okay, back then everyone looked like a hippie. As was the custom, Jesus stood up to read. The scroll of the prophet Isaiah was handed to Him. The synagogue people weren't expecting anything new, just the comforting structure of the familiar: the ancient promises of the prophets, the assurance that they were the chosen people, and the confidence that God was on their side.

And then the words came rolling down like thunder:

> The Spirit of the Lord is on me,
> because he has anointed me
> to proclaim good news to the poor.
> He has sent me to proclaim freedom for the
> prisoners
> and recovery of sight for the blind,
> to set the oppressed free,
> to proclaim the year of the Lord's favor.[2]

Then Jesus took it further. The good news He was announcing wasn't just for the good people sitting in the synagogue, He said. It was for foreigners, non-Jews, and outsiders. The gospel wasn't about life-as-usual comfort for the holy club. It was a revolution.

This did not go over well with Jesus's first-century friends in Nazareth. They rose up in a fury, hustled Him out of their synagogue, and tried to kill Him.

It wasn't as if Christians in mid-1960s American churchianity wanted their churches to be exclusive clubs. Believers earnestly wanted their families and friends and neighbors to come to know Jesus. But still, many churches were homogenous bastions of clean-cut social externals, not always focused on being open communities of love and good news for the poor, sight for the blind, and freedom for the oppressed.

But something was about to happen, right in 1960s America, and right in Chuck Smith's little, but growing, church.

In the words of another Old Testament prophet, Joel, old men were dreaming dreams, young men were seeing visions, and God was about to pour out His Spirit on His servants, both men and women.[3] The result would be a spiritual earthquake.

———

Most people know about earthquakes and their aftershocks. Foreshocks are less familiar. They're the phenomena that herald the arrival of an actual quake (which is known, of course, as the mainshock). Some scientists believe that foreshocks are part of the earth's process prior to nucleation. A small event triggers a larger one, then a larger one, cascading toward the big one. Other models show that foreshocks relieve the stress of the actual earthquake before it arrives.

Perhaps the mid-1960s was a time of foreshocks. The big eruptions in US culture hadn't quite peaked yet, but the tectonic plates of social norms were shifting, and the friction was growing stronger. Even as thousands of pastors like Chuck Smith were faithfully preaching the gospel in their churches across America, the serene 1950s landscape of American faith and culture was groaning and changing. Some sort of earthquake was coming.

The first blip on the cultural seismometer involved the Beatles. No surprise there. On March 4, 1966, a British writer named Maureen Cleave interviewed John Lennon at his Tudor home outside London. Lennon's house was outfitted with concert memorabilia, posters, black carpeting and purple wallpaper, a full-size crucifix, a gorilla costume, a large Mickey Mouse doll, a medieval suit of armor, and an extensive library. Lennon had works by Alfred, Lord Tennyson, Jonathan Swift, Oscar Wilde, George Orwell, and Aldous Huxley, as well as the Tibetan Book of the Dead and the 1965 bestseller *The Passover Plot*. The last hypothesizes, among other things, that Jesus meticulously planned His life and crucifixion to reflect Old Testament prophecies. Then He orchestrated a plot to be drugged on the cross so He could be taken down before He actually died and then revived later by His friends. (This plan was foiled by the Roman soldier's spear to His side.)

Lennon had been reflecting on religion, and in the course of Cleave's interview, he said in passing:

> Christianity will go. It will vanish and shrink. I needn't argue about that; I'm right and I'll be proved right. We're more popular than Jesus now; I don't know which will go first—rock 'n' roll or Christianity. Jesus was all right but his disciples were thick and ordinary. It's them twisting it that ruins it for me.[4]

When the interview was published in Great Britain, there was little response. A few months later, however, a US teen magazine called *Datebook* quoted the comments, and there were violent reactions from mainstream America. Protests broke out; some radio stations stopped playing the Beatles' songs. Churches and civic groups sponsored public burnings of the group's albums. An Alabama radio station urged listeners to send their Beatles records and paraphernalia to the station to be destroyed with an industrial grade tree-grinding machine temporarily known as the "Beatle-grinder."

These protests came at the same time as the Beatles' US tour in August 1966. Activists with signs proclaiming "Jesus loves you, do the Beatles?" and "Beatles, go home!" showed up at press conferences. John Lennon bitterly remarked that he should have just said "television is more popular than Jesus" and he would have gotten away with it. Paul McCartney called the outcry "hysterical, low-grade American thinking,"[5] and a lot of young people agreed with him.

Still, commercial concerns—as in concert and record sales—demanded that John Lennon make an apology, which he did. Sort of. But the hysteria led, in part, to the Beatles' weary decision to quit touring. They could pursue new creative heights as a studio-only band and not have to bother with the stubborn whims of the mainstream.

Around the same time, progressive theologians weren't too worried about whether Jesus or the Beatles were more popular. They had a different axe to grind, one that was popularized on the cover of *Time* magazine. In dramatic red and black graphics, the magazine called out to people from the newsstands, "Is God Dead?"

In 1966, this was a shocking public question. American civil religion had been alive and well for decades, and people who had no personal relationship with God fondly regarded Him as American as apple pie and the Fourth of July. Nonetheless, *Time* reported, "a small band of radical theologians has seriously argued that the churches accept the fact of God's death and get along without him."[6]

An additional 1966 development showed, for those who noticed, yet another rip in the fabric of the cultural religion that had buoyed America through the 1950s. In San Francisco, a former circus performer named Anton LaVey founded the Church of Satan.

LaVey might as well have come from Central Casting. He shaved his head—this was back when no one shaved their heads and most cool people were trying to grow their hair down to their ankles—and wore a black goatee. He posed for photos with snakes, capes, and pentagrams, and lived in an all-black Victorian house with special rooms set aside for black masses.

A book called *The Devil's Party* noted that "LaVey created a belief system somewhere between religion, philosophy, psychology, and carnival (or circus), freely appropriating science, mythology, fringe beliefs, and play in a potent mix."[7]

During his circus days, LaVey had specialized in magic and hypnosis. He was entertaining; it's no surprise that a sprinkling of Hollywood entertainers, like Sammy Davis Jr. and Jayne Mansfield, along with hippies and other curious counterculturalists, came to his gatherings. After Mansfield was nearly decapitated in an awful late-night car crash in 1967, some said that LaVey had cursed her.

LaVey confided to a friendly neighborhood pastor named Ed Plowman that practitioners of actual, supernatural Satanism were in fact "nut cases." He told Ed that he was an atheist, using Satan as a symbol to help people deal with guilt-ridden consciences. Nevertheless, LaVey knew how to butter his bread. He wrote a number of books, including his Satanic Bible, was a regular on the talk show circuit in the late '60s and '70s, fell into financial difficulties as his dark star waned, and eventually faded from the scene.

These 1966 cultural cracks in America's wholesome façade—Lennon's claim, *Time* magazine's question, and the temporary popularity of a guy like Anton LaVey—all pointed to something that was actually positive, at its root.

Many Americans were no longer willing to swallow conventional churchianity that was just part of a God-and-country type of mind-set. Established, easy-answer norms were cracking, and some were even crashing down. Some people, like Anton LaVey, were just cynical mutineers, of course. But many cultural revolutionaries—and the millions of young people who followed them—were sincerely searching. They longed for what was true, real, and transformational.

The question was, would their search take them on the wide, bright highway with the abrupt dead end, or to a narrower path that in fact led to a whole new life?

5

The Be-In, the Summer of Love, and a Nudist Vegetarian Hippie

A lost child has been delivered to the stage, and is now being cared for by the Hells Angels.

Random public service announcement from the stage during the Be-In

With LSD, we experienced what it took Tibetan monks 20 years to obtain, yet we got there in 20 minutes.

Luria Castell Dickson, a '60s San Francisco student, activist, and musician, quoted in *Vanity Fair*

Greg Laurie wasn't interested in the Church of Satan or in liberal theologians pontificating on the death of God. Greg wasn't into cultural analysis. Nor had he ever heard of Pastor Chuck Smith; he wasn't in the habit of making acquaintance with members of the clergy. He did wonder about God now and then, but he was a teenager, more interested in fitting in at school and trying to figure out what kind of a life he wanted.

The one thing he did know is he didn't want the life his mother was living.

At the time, he was at Corona del Mar High School in Newport Beach, California. There were Porsches in the parking lot; most of his fellow students had two parents at home who bought them clothes, school supplies, cars, and whatever they needed. Greg could not imagine what that was like. He got a job as a busboy and stretched his pay so he could buy a few brand-name shirts and pants. He rotated them carefully so he wouldn't repeat an outfit during the week and could fit in with the unofficial dress code at his upscale high school.

Because he was funny and sarcastic, the upper-class cool crowd welcomed Greg, even though he was a lowly freshman. Next thing he knew he was drinking and smoking at parties. He hated the taste of alcohol, but he'd force it down so he could get a buzz. Booze made him feel like less of an observer and more of a participant.

But there was a problem. One night he had a little out-of-body experience, so to speak, and saw himself in a clump of boring people at a party, trying to get the girls to laugh and the guys to think he was cool, standing under a palm tree with a drink in one hand and a cigarette in the other. He realized he looked just like someone he'd seen in similar scenes way too often. He looked just like his mother. He was turning into Charlene 2.0.

That moment of disgusted self-awareness made Greg decide to go with something new. It was time to throw over the alcohol, the preppy look, and the teenaged version of old adult vices. It was time to get into new vices. Clearly, drugs were the answer.

Right about the same time, Northern California was treated to an influx of young people with the same outlook as Greg, though they were a few years older. It was 1967's Human Be-In, where the cream of hippie culture got together in Golden Gate Park to, yes, celebrate being human.

You could call it the ultimate selfie festival, even though selfies wouldn't really be invented until people's arms grew longer with the advent of the iPhone.

The Be-In started as a protest to the outlawing of LSD, which had been belatedly accomplished by the US government in late 1966, after the genie had been out of the bottle for quite some time. It began with a call to order, though that is definitely the wrong term, in the form of some fairly long-winded Hindu chanting from poet Alan Ginsberg.

Ginsberg was followed by speeches from other poets, countercultural gurus, and bands like the Grateful Dead and Jefferson Airplane, among others. Members of the notorious motorcycle gang the Hells Angels were brought in to provide security and to tenderly take care of lost children. Former Harvard professor and LSD evangelist Timothy Leary speechified his usual marching orders for the younger generation: "Tune in, turn on, and drop out."

Thirty thousand mystics, political radicals who hated the Vietnam War, Marxists, pacifists, and other young people took it all in. It was an extravaganza, with drums, incense, chimes, banners, feathers, candles, flutes, animals, cymbals, and dancing. People were dressed in miniskirts, peasant blouses, top hats, Edwardian trousers, tie-dyed T-shirts, velvet cloaks, body paint, or nothing at all. Vast clouds of smoke hung over the park; you could get high just sitting there. Seventy-five twenty-pound turkeys were distributed, along with generous servings of free "White Lightning" LSD cooked up for the event by a philanthropic underground chemist.

The Be-In got great publicity across the country, and soon San Francisco was the place to be in. Young people climbed into their VW bugs with flower power stickers, or hopped on a Greyhound bus, or stuck out their thumbs on the highway, and made their way to San Francisco, the mecca of the hippie movement. Spring turned to summer, and John Phillips of the Mamas & the Papas released "San Francisco (Be Sure to Wear Some Flowers in Your Hair)," sung by Scott McKenzie.

About seventy-five thousand young people heard the call, and soon San Francisco was overflowing with hippies everywhere.

As *Vanity Fair* described it,

> The Summer of Love . . . thrust a new kind of music—acid rock—across the airwaves, nearly put barbers out of business, traded clothes for costumes, turned psychedelic drugs into sacred door keys. . . . It turned sex with strangers into a mode of generosity, made "uptight" an epithet on a par with "racist," refashioned the notion of earnest Peace Corps idealism into a bacchanalian rhapsody, and set that favorite American adjective, "free," on a fresh altar.[1]

There were all kinds of people there, some who would later be part of the Jesus Revolution . . . and some who would not.

A drifter named Charles Manson was older than most of the kids who showed up for the Summer of Love. He was thirty-two years old, a career criminal who had just been released from prison. Manson had been divorced twice and fathered at least two abandoned sons. He was a pimp and a car thief who considered himself a musical genius. The son of a teenaged prostitute, he'd grown up on the streets, and somewhere along the way Manson had started developing a fluid theology that blended his own messianic complex with Eastern mysticism, the oneness of the universe, and equal-opportunity copulation with like-minded disciples, both male and female.

In April of '67, Manson had moved in with a woman named Mary Brunner. In May he picked up an eighteen-year-old girl on Venice Beach and brought her home to Mary. He'd later nickname her "Squeaky" from the noises she made when he'd pimp her out to other men. By the Summer of Love, Charles Manson had already added various other runaways and needy young women looking for love to his "family."

One of the younger people who floated into San Francisco that summer was a seventeen-year-old art student named Lonnie Frisbee. Lonnie was from Southern California and had dropped out of high school there to enroll in art school in San Francisco.

Lonnie told his friends he'd had an awful childhood. His biological father was a serial adulterer, a drunk who beat Lonnie and his mom and eventually left her for another woman. Lonnie's mother tracked down the other woman's husband and eventually married him. The new stepdad hated and rejected Lonnie and his brothers. Then, beginning at age eight, Lonnie was sexually molested by a seventeen-year-old guy from the neighborhood who babysat for the family. The adults in Lonnie's life did not believe his story.

There was one bright spot: a godly grandmother who took Lonnie to church and encouraged him to dream. So, though he'd been born with clubfoot, he dreamed of being a Mouseketeer and dancing on television. (This was a common childhood dream back then; the Mouseketeers, mascots of the shiny new Disney empire, were the happiest, perkiest, coolest kids on TV.) As a teenager Lonnie worked on his dance moves, and his dreams almost came true when he was recruited to be a regular dancer on a local afternoon TV show that featured live bands. It was called *Shebang*, and it was as groovy as afternoon TV could get.

Lonnie got into drugs in his early teens, first acid and other hallucinogens, then dope. (He was initially scared to try marijuana because of a drug deterrent film called *Reefer Madness* that was routinely shown in the public schools. Anyone who took the movie's message to heart knew that dope was the certain doorway to death, destruction, and insanity.)

But eventually Lonnie succumbed to reefer madness as well as the madness of every other drug on the streets, which was saying a lot. He went out to the desert, tripping, looking for UFOs. He protested the Vietnam War, hitchhiked up and down the coast of California, and spent a lot of time seeking God in a canyon near Palm Springs. One time he and a hundred of his closest friends were arrested for doing so, only because they were all naked and smoking dope at the time.

So in 1967, Lonnie Frisbee was just another vegetarian nudist druggie on the scene. But that was about to change, and he would become a key figure in California's Jesus Movement.

During that same summer of '67, the Beatles released their watershed album, *Sgt. Pepper's Lonely Hearts Club Band.* It's hard to overstate how significant that album was for music lovers in the '60s. In its rundown of the five hundred greatest albums of all time, *Rolling Stone* called it "the most important rock & roll album ever made, an unsurpassed adventure in concept, sound, songwriting, cover art and studio technology by the greatest rock & roll group of all time . . . the pinnacle of the Beatles' eight years as recording artists."[2]

The album was also the final break with the boy-band Beatles as cultural icons. "We were fed up with being Beatles," Paul McCartney said later. The four suit-wearing lads on the *Ed Sullivan Show*—memorialized as stiff wax figures on the album's crowded cover—were gone forever.

Rolling Stone concluded, "*Sgt. Pepper* defined the opulent revolutionary optimism of psychedelia and instantly spread the gospel of love, acid, Eastern spirituality and electric guitars around the globe. No other pop record of that era, or since, has had such an immediate, titanic impact."[3]

Greg Laurie didn't know how history or *Rolling Stone* would judge the impact of *Sgt. Pepper*. But like his peers everywhere, he'd sit in his bedroom and listen to it for hours. He'd stare at that iconic album cover plastered with cutouts of everyone from Karl Marx to David Livingstone to W. C. Fields to Shirley Temple, and wonder what it all *meant*. It was the first album ever to print the lyrics on the cover. It felt like if you just smoked enough weed and stared long enough at those words, you'd enter through a portal to some higher level of understanding.

By this point, Greg had made his move from preppy culture to hippie culture. He'd transferred to Harbor High School. He grew his hair out, wore hippie clothes, and purposefully hung out with a low-level outcast group rather than cloning and connecting with the cool kids. It freed him from the pressure of having to make a persona or play by anyone else's rules.

Like Lonnie Frisbee and everybody else in that era, Greg had seen the films in his public high school warning about the madness of marijuana. The message was that kids flipped out and went crazy on the stuff. Greg had tried it; he hadn't flipped out. So, like everything else that adults said, the film must have been a lie. *They lie to us about pot*, he thought. *They lie about Vietnam. What's the use of even listening to them?*

At the time, though, Greg had a sense of right and wrong that had come from somewhere. For example, he knew it was wrong to lie; that's why it bugged him so much when adults did it. And he knew that what he saw at home just wasn't right. There were pornographic magazines littering the house, his mom sleeping off hangovers, and random men in and out. It didn't take a genius to realize all that just wasn't healthy or right.

Sometimes Greg would come home late at night, high, and Charlene would be slouched in the living room, drunk, smoking a cigarette dangling with ash. He'd sit down, his eyes red and glassy, and they'd have a "conversation." It just seemed so ironic to Greg. *She doesn't even know I'm stoned out of my mind*, he'd think. *At least I know I'm out of it. And she just keeps pretending she's fine.*

Down deep, he was a romantic. He wanted the opposite of his mother's long-term fog and short-term stands. It sounded too sappy in his brain to even articulate, really, but what he wanted was true love. He wanted a relationship that was unique, permanent, and actually fulfilling.

Meanwhile, most of his friends were sex fiends. They constantly bugged him about girls: Was he out there scoring?

Why not? What was wrong with him? One guy in particular would not leave him alone. "Look," he said to Greg one day, "why don't you just take my girlfriend and do it with her? She's up for it!"

Greg hated the idea; it just seemed so impersonal. But he had to get his friends off his back about the whole sex thing. So one night, after smoking enough dope to knock out an elephant, he got together with a girl he'd just met. Later, he remembered very little about that not-so-special night.

All he knew was that this was not how it was supposed to be. He was longing for something he had never seen but he knew must exist. Somewhere.

6

Miracle in the Middle East

The existence of Israel is an error which must be rectified. This is our opportunity to wipe out the ignominy which has been with us since 1948. *Our goal is clear—to wipe Israel off the map.*

President Aref of Iraq, May 31, 1967

I believe that what we're seeing in the world today is the fulfillment of these ancient prophecies written between 2,000 and 3,500 years ago. As the world staggers from one crisis to another, I believe that we're racing on a countdown to the end of history as we know it.

Hal Lindsey, *The Late, Great Planet Earth*

The summer of 1967 was also the setting for one of the most dramatic conflicts in twentieth-century history, Israel's Six-Day War. Aside from its strategic geopolitical importance—interpreted in a variety of ways—Israel's astonishing war in the land of Abraham had direct repercussions for the budding

Jesus Revolution in America. Chuck Smith, in particular, tied the war directly into Old Testament prophecies and the end times; it galvanized his urgency to spread the gospel.

Ever since its establishment as a nation in 1948, Israel had been threatened on all sides by its Arab neighbors. Its War for Independence had concluded with a cease-fire that left Jerusalem divided in two. The entire Old City, including the Temple Mount, the Western Wall, and other holy sites, had been put under the control of the Jordanians. Jews were not allowed to enter Jerusalem's walls or pray inside the city.

In the late 1940s and early 1950s, Egypt had blockaded the Suez Canal and the Straits of Tiran to shipping destined for Israel. In 1956, a United Nations emergency force was deployed in the Sinai Peninsula, and the straits were reopened. But by the late spring of 1967, President Nasser of Egypt had again closed the waterways to Israeli vessels, evicted the UN peacekeepers, and mobilized troops along his border with Israel.

"Our basic objective will be the destruction of Israel," President Nasser declared.[1] The chairman of the Palestine Liberation Organization described the impending fate of the Jews in Israel: "I estimate that none of them will survive."[2]

Egypt and Syria activated a mutual defense pact, and Syria massed troops on its forty-mile border with Israel. The Syrians occupied the high ground, including the area known as the Golan Heights, which the Syrians had been fortifying for eighteen years. Meanwhile, the nation of Jordan had deployed ten of its eleven brigades to defend its densely populated territory on the West Bank, as well as the Old City of Jerusalem, with its Temple Mount and other holy places that had long been denied to the Jews.

The tension grew. The Soviet Union knew that Israel's ally, the United States, was preoccupied with the ongoing debacle in Vietnam. The USSR disseminated a fair amount of disinformation, fueling the fire in the Arab world. President Johnson publicly urged caution and appealed for the Middle East to find solutions aside from war.

With hostile forces amassed on his borders, Meir Amit, the enterprising head of Mossad, Israel's spy agency, flew to Washington, DC, in disguise, using a false passport. His country had to move forward, he told President Johnson's Secretary of Defense, Robert McNamara. Almost all Israeli men under the age of fifty were mobilized for war. The dark jokes among them were that the last one to go should not forget to turn out the lights, or that after the war all the Jews left in Israel would fit in a single phone booth. Their enemies were pressing in.

"I read you loud and clear," McNamara responded.

Amit took that as the implicit approval of the United States of America. He and the Israeli ambassador flew back to Tel Aviv in an airplane full of gas masks.

On the morning of June 5, 1967, small groups of Israeli jets took off from bases in their homeland. Their Air Force had amassed extensive reconnaissance of every air base in Egypt, Jordan, and Syria. The pilots cleared their country's airspace and flew fifty feet above the Mediterranean Sea. They knew that their Egyptian counterparts were on alert at dawn, but now, at 7:45 a.m., most senior Egyptian military and political leaders would be caught in Cairo's notorious traffic jams and thus would be out of touch. (Though cellular communications have improved immensely since 1967, Cairo's traffic has not.)

Still, Egyptian officers based at the radar station in northern Jordan did pick up the scrambling Israeli aircraft. They sent a red alert message to Cairo. The sergeant in the decoding room of the supreme command there tried but failed to decipher the message using the usual code. He neglected to note that a new code had been put in place the day before.

Israeli pilots bombed more than three hundred Egyptian fighter planes and rendered runways throughout the country unusable. In separate raids, their brother pilots took out two-thirds of the Syrian air power and most of the Royal Jordanian Air Force. Israeli ground troops took on the Egyptian army forces in the Sinai Peninsula, the Syrians in the Golan Heights, and the Jordanians in the West Bank and East Jerusalem.

On June 11 a cease-fire was signed. Israel lost less than one thousand fighters, while the Arab forces lost twenty thousand troops. For the first time in almost two millennia the Jewish holy places in Jerusalem were under the control of Jews. Israelis considered it a miracle of biblical proportions. Israel had crushed her enemies to the north, east, and south, and tripled her territory.

President Nasser of Egypt resigned, but was persuaded to remain in office after millions of his citizens protested in the streets. He served as Egypt's president until his death in 1970 and was succeeded by Anwar Sadat, who would later be assassinated by his own troops for signing a peace treaty with Israel.

King Hussein of Jordan lost East Jerusalem for a time, but kept his throne. He made peace with Israel in 1994.

And in Syria, the air force commander who had been in the ruling junta seized sole power in 1970. His name was Hafez al-Assad. He died in 2000 . . . and his son, Bashar al-Assad, bled and bullied the region, massacring innocents from the day he took on his father's reins of power.

The Six-Day War was not the last word, by any means, in Israel's complicated history and the anguishing issues surrounding her borders for both Israelis and Palestinians. But at that moment in time, many American Christians saw the war's conclusion as a fulfillment of biblical end times prophecy. Even as academics scoffed, preachers told stories of angels defending Israeli troops and guiding their artillery. For the nation of Israel to face—and crush—the much bigger armies of the Arab world was a modern-day David and Goliath story and a signal that human history was drawing to completion. Recapturing Jerusalem for the first time in two thousand years seemed to be a direct fulfillment of Luke 21:24: "Jerusalem will be trampled on by the Gentiles *until the times of the Gentiles are fulfilled*" (emphasis added).

Some commentators pointed to complex prophecies in Daniel 8 that looked ahead to Alexander the Great's defeat of the Persian Empire in 334 BC.[3] Daniel's vision went on to describe a timeline of 2,300 "evenings and mornings" from that Gentile occupation until Jerusalem would be freed from the control of foreign nations. Many Christians, applying the time scale that one day equals one year (see Ezek. 4:6), and bearing in mind that there is no date 0 AD, did the math and saw the fulfillment of Daniel's vision in—you guessed it—1967.

At Calvary Chapel in Costa Mesa, California, 7,586 miles from Jerusalem, the Six-Day War was not just some faraway news story for Pastor Chuck Smith. He started a special Bible class on Israel and biblical prophecy. His church had not yet grown in the ways that it would in just a few years, but Chuck preached and taught his flock with a new urgency: the Bible was true, its interpretation of human history was real and relevant, Jesus was going to return soon, and evangelism and discipleship were more vital and imperative than ever in these "last days" that were now upon the citizens of Earth, circa 1967.

7

1968

And the Wind Began to Howl

Even in our sleep, pain which cannot forget falls drop by drop upon the heart until, in our own despair, against our will, comes wisdom through the awful grace of God.

Robert F. Kennedy, quoting the Greek poet Aeschylus, after the assassination of Martin Luther King Jr.

After San Francisco's Summer of Love in 1967, its hippie subculture became a hub for curious tourists. Middle-aged sightseers came in buses, Kodak cameras around their necks, to gawk at the flower children and take their pictures. The infamous Psychedelic Shop on Haight Street closed in protest; its owners moved back to the Midwest.

A lot of the summer hippies went back to school. Others who stayed found that the bloom was off the rose. The bright idealism of the early days faded to a darker scene: malnutrition, overdoses, cold street corners, junkies, and dirty needles. Free love had been generous: many kids were suffering from ugly sexually transmitted diseases. Some of the flower children went on LSD trips and never came back. Others got hungry and sick.

A well-known neighborhood acid dealer named Shob was found stabbed to death, his right arm severed. Police stopped another drug dealer and found the bloody arm behind the seat of his peace-sign decorated van. Crime was up; maybe the hippie dream had been confiscated. At any rate, utopia's bright colors had gone gray.

At the end of the summer, George Harrison visited Haight-Ashbury with his wife, the model Pattie Boyd. Wearing granny glasses in the shape of hearts, the Beatle strolled the streets, looking for action. Eventually some of the hippies recognized him and a crowd formed . . . but the San Fran experience wasn't quite what George had in mind. He said later he thought it would be more upscale. "I expected them to all own their own little shops. I expected them all to be nice and clean and friendly and happy."[1]

Sadly for George, San Francisco's hippies didn't own cute little shops, and they evidently hadn't had access to anti-acne products. He said they were "hideous, spotty little teenagers."

For their part, the pimpled hippies following their Beatle down the magical mystery streets said George was too stoned to even play the guitar someone handed him. His biographer wrote that George ended up being chased back to his limousine by a "wild band of jeering hippies."[2]

Not too long after Lonnie Frisbee's summer of '67 arrest for public nudity and drug possession, he hit his favorite canyon again, this time without a hundred of his closest friends. His brain was an urgent swirl, full of the beauty around him, questions about the meaning of life, half-remembered threads of everything he'd experienced over his eighteen years, and a nice tab of LSD.

As Lonnie would later explain it, he took off all his clothes, turned his face to the sky, and screamed toward Heaven, "Jesus, if you're really real, reveal yourself to me!"[3]

He felt the atmosphere around him begin to tingle, shimmer, and glow. He was terrified. He felt the presence of God. He saw visions. He felt God's calling on his life.

Lonnie returned to San Francisco, and though there are different versions about what happened next, he evidently met some Jesus People on the street in the fall of 1967. They were part of a small community of former hippies and druggies who had come to know Christ and enthusiastically surrendered everything to Him. They lived in community, modeling a New Testament family of believers, and were loosely headed by a couple named Ted and Liz Wise.

By all accounts, the Wises were strategically used by God to spark the embers of what became the Jesus Movement in Northern and Southern California. They had been enthusiastic drug devotees, "pre-hippies" coming out of a bohemian Beat lifestyle in the early '60s. They had both come to know Christ, gotten rooted—with a fair amount of cross-cultural confusion—in a "square" local church, and grown in their understanding of the Scriptures.

By mid-1967 they'd started a storefront-type outreach in the Haight, reaching out to the hippies who were flooding the city. A lot of these young people were finding that the hippie life in Haight-Ashbury was not all sweetness and light. Girls were getting raped, kids were strung out, and the hippie experience was short on real health for either body or soul. The Wises would feed them, tell them about Jesus, and give them paperback copies of a new translation of the New Testament called *Good News for Modern Man*. Many of those lost kids embraced the good news. And some did not: a short hippie named Charlie Manson would come in, eat soup, and jam on a borrowed guitar. He didn't want to hear about Jesus; he thought he *was* Jesus.

When Ted Wise encountered Lonnie Frisbee on the street one day, Lonnie was evidently preaching Jesus, UFOs, and Christ consciousness. He told Ted how he'd experienced the reality of God in the canyon a few weeks earlier. Ted discerned that his head had gotten a little messed up with drugs, and his theology was just a little mixed up too. He took him home, fed him, and invited him to come and live with the community. Lonnie studied the Bible with them, and over time embraced a more orthodox understanding of the gospel.[4]

On October 7, 1967, the Haight's hardcore flower children proclaimed the official end of San Francisco as hippie mecca. They conducted a mock funeral, solemnly mourning "the death of the hippie, devoted son of mass media." Organizers said they wanted to let young people know that this was the end of the San Fran movement, and don't come here; they should stay home and bring the revolution to where they lived. Pallbearers carried a wooden coffin draped in black. It was filled with psychedelic posters, bongs, kazoos, Zen manuals, and beads.

The Summer of Love had passed, and winter was coming.

A few weeks after the symbolic hippie funeral in San Francisco, the biggest antiwar demonstration yet took place on the other side of the country. One hundred thousand protesters gathered at the Lincoln Memorial in Washington, DC. Author Norman Mailer was among those who got arrested; Benjamin Spock, the best-known pediatrician in America, denounced President Johnson in his speech as the crowd booed and cheered. Later that evening, around thirty thousand of the protesters marched on the Pentagon, where brutal confrontations with soldiers ended in hundreds of arrests.

Back in November 1967, half a million American soldiers were in Vietnam. The draft system was calling forty thousand young men into the service each month. It was the first war with news coverage in real time: television reports were showing, in living color, young men under fire in a jungle far away. More than one hundred thousand troops had been wounded and more than fifteen thousand killed so far. Coffins were coming home to America.

At the end of January 1968, a cease-fire was declared between the People's Army of North Vietnam and the South Vietnamese and American troops. It was a temporary lull so the Vietnamese people could celebrate their sacred new year, which they called *Tet*. Thousands of soldiers were on leave. Civilians took to the streets in Saigon and other cities, shooting off firecrackers and fireworks.

In the midst of the week-long festivities, however, thousands of Vietcong soldiers made their way into key cities in the South. Some wore civilian clothes and mingled with the populace, testing their weapons while fireworks exploded. Some wore stolen South Vietnamese army uniforms. And though officials had not noticed the unusual number of funeral processions taking place in previous weeks, now it became apparent that Vietcong had not only infiltrated the

South but had also smuggled thousands of weapons in those coffins that had slowly moved through the streets.

The Tet Offensive—one of the most famous and horrific campaigns in modern military history—exploded throughout South Vietnam with massacres, ambushes, assassinations, and thousands of civilian casualties. War correspondents flooded US outlets with terrible reports of carnage.

The communists sustained enormous losses in their surprise attack, but it was a turning point for their cause. For the first time, many who supported US involvement in Vietnam confessed that this was a war America would not win. Wounded American veterans threw away their war medals. Student protesters took over academic buildings on their campuses.

On March 31, 1968, President Lyndon Johnson's televised speech to the nation ended with a surprise: "I shall not seek, and I will not accept, the nomination of my party for another term as your president," he said.

Polling at the time showed that Johnson would defeat any political rivals. Those closest to him knew the real reason for his decision not to run. Vietnam. Even as early as March 1965, the White House taping system had recorded Johnson's assessment: "The great trouble I'm under—a man can fight if he can see daylight down the road somewhere. But there ain't no daylight in Vietnam."[5]

The stubborn war had drained the tough Texas politician. Johnson's father and grandfather had both died at age sixty-four; the president had a premonition he would do the same. Four years after his announcement that he wouldn't run again for the presidency, Johnson would die of a heart attack at his ranch in Texas—at age sixty-four.

Meanwhile, protests also continued for the domestic focus of the day, civil rights for African Americans. It had been nearly five long years since Dr. Martin Luther King Jr.'s spine-tingling "I Have a Dream" speech to a quarter of a million people at the Lincoln Memorial, in which he called for an absolute end to racism and for civil and economic rights for African Americans.

"I have a dream," Dr. King had thundered back in 1963.

A dream that this nation will rise up and live out the true meaning of its creed: "We hold these truths to be self-evident: that all men are created equal."

I have a dream that my four little children will one day live in a nation where they will not be judged by the color of their skin but by the content of their character.

I have a dream that one day every valley shall be exalted, every hill and mountain shall be made low, the rough places will be made plain, and the crooked places will be made straight, and the glory of the Lord shall be revealed, and all flesh shall see it together.[6]

It was a beautiful dream, full of hope, even in the face of formidable odds back in 1963.

Now it was April 3, 1968. Dr. King was in a church in Memphis, Tennessee, supporting a sanitation workers' strike. He talked about the daunting trials of the ongoing battle for civil rights, of his disappointment that a nation conceived in liberty for all would still be home to injustice for some. But still, there was hope for all, even if some did not make it to the end of the journey. He ended his speech with reflections full of Old Testament imagery and personal peace, prescient words that have stunned us all ever since.

Well, I don't know what will happen now. We've got some difficult days ahead. But it doesn't matter with me now. . . . Like anybody, I would like to live a long life. Longevity has its place. But I'm not concerned about that now. I just want to do God's will. And He's allowed me to go up to the mountain. And I've looked over. And I've *seen* the Promised Land. I may not get there with you. But I want you to know tonight, that we, as a people, will get to the Promised Land!

And so I'm happy tonight. I'm not worried about anything. I'm not fearing any man. My eyes have seen the glory of the coming of the Lord![7]

At six o'clock the next evening, Martin Luther King and several of his colleagues stepped out onto the balcony of their Memphis motel. As they talked about their planned rally that evening, Dr. King asked their musician to play the old Negro spiritual, "Take My Hand, Precious Lord."

"Play it real pretty," he said with a grin.

There was a single shot. An explosion; 156 decibels. Louder than a jet engine. A .30-caliber bullet ripped through King's right cheek. It broke his jaw and several vertebrae, severed his jugular vein, and blew off his necktie. He fell to the floor in a pool of blood. His friends rushed him to the hospital. And an hour later, King entered into that Promised Land he had seen so clearly the night before.

Rioting, burning, and looting broke out in more than one hundred cities across the United States. Parts of Washington, DC, erupted in flames. Radicals called for retribution and armed resistance, fueling the growth of the Black Power movement and the Black Panther Party. Hundreds of thousands of people, black and white, mourned the "apostle of nonviolence," as President Johnson called the slain civil rights leader.

Senator Robert Kennedy, campaigning for the Democratic nomination to run for president of the United States, was in Indianapolis when he heard of Dr. King's death.

"Oh, God," he moaned. "When is this violence going to stop?"[8]

It fell to Kennedy to give the news to the huge crowd that had turned out to hear him that evening. He spoke for less than five minutes from a podium mounted on a flatbed truck. The people screamed and wept and wailed as he spoke of the fallen civil rights leader. Then he did what he'd never done before, and spoke publicly of his own brother's murder.

> For those of you who are black and are tempted to be filled with hatred and distrust at the injustice of such an act, against all white people, I can only say that I feel in my own heart that same kind of feeling. I had a member of my family killed, but he was killed by a white man. But we have to make an effort . . . to go beyond these rather difficult times. . . .
>
> The vast majority of white people and the vast majority of black people in this country want to live together, want to improve the quality of our life, and want justice for all human beings who abide in our land. Let us dedicate ourselves to what the Greeks wrote so many years ago: to tame the savageness of man and make gentle the life of this world.[9]

The crowd wept but did not erupt into violence. People quietly went on their way. In spite of rioting in cities like Chicago, New York, Detroit, Oakland, and Pittsburgh—with thirty-five killed and twenty-five hundred injured—Indianapolis was calm that night.

Two months after Dr. King's murder, on the night of June 4, 1968, Robert Kennedy won the California Democratic presidential primary. Just after midnight on the morning of June 5, he'd addressed his supporters at the Ambassador Hotel in Los Angeles. He was planning to go to a later meeting in another part of the building, but aides changed the plan and instead escorted him through the hotel kitchen on his way to an impromptu press conference with members of the media.

Surrounded by aides, Kennedy made his way through a narrow passageway. There was a steam table on one side and an ice machine on the other. A seventeen-year-old busboy in a white jacket caught Senator Kennedy's eye. His name was Juan Romero, and he'd served the senator a meal earlier that day. The senator recognized the teenager and stopped to shake his hand.

Suddenly, a dark-haired man with a gun stepped out from behind the ice machine and lunged toward Kennedy. He shot him three times and sprayed bullets into the crowd until he was tackled by the senator's aides and friends, five of whom were wounded.

Reporters, photographers, and colleagues rushed the scene. One journalist snapped the photo that became the iconic image of the day: Senator Kennedy is splayed on his back, his legs at odd angles. The young busboy, Juan Romero, in his white service jacket, squats by Kennedy's side. His face is blurred with fear and confusion as he cradles his hero's broken head. He's already ripped his rosary out of his pocket and placed it in Kennedy's open palm. Kennedy's eyes are open; he is still alive.

The senator had taken three bullets. One exited from his chest, one lodged in his neck, and another had torn through his brain. In spite of frantic surgeries and efforts to save his life, he died twenty-six hours after the shooting. His assassin, a Palestinian radical named Sirhan Sirhan, would later say that he killed Robert Kennedy because the senator had supported Israel in the Arab-Israeli War of 1967. Sirhan was apprehended, tried, and sentenced to death, though his sentence would later be commuted to life in prison.

RFK was forty-two years old when he died. For many young people, particularly in the wake of Martin Luther King's death, Kennedy had represented their last hope for social justice, racial tolerance, and an end to the war in Vietnam. Maybe the teenaged busboy, Juan Romero, said it best. His hero's assassination "made me realize that no matter how much hope you have, it can be taken away in a second."[10]

In 1968, Greg Laurie was fifteen years old. He already knew that hope could be taken away in a second. But he hadn't really placed much confidence in political heroes like Robert Kennedy or Martin Luther King Jr. Like everyone, he was shocked and horrified by their deaths. And like most young people, he hated the war in Vietnam.

But also like that of most teenagers, Greg's world was pretty small. His lack of hope wasn't played out on some grand, national stage. It came from his own story. His cynicism wasn't focused on sticking it to "the Man" or the Establishment. It came from his mom, and from not one man but a whole parade of men in her life. He didn't trust adults. In his experience, they lied; they did what they wanted and left their mess. He'd clean his mother up when she passed out. He'd walk past her open bedroom door and see her naked on the bed with some guy he didn't even know. He'd hear her slosh and slur how much she loved him, then yell at him in the next boozy breath. When she was drunk, she couldn't even say his name right.

Greg was on his own.

He was excited, though, when the Newport Pop Festival came to his area in the beginning of August 1968. It was the first music concert ever to have more than one hundred thousand paid attendees, and it was going to be a phenomenon. He didn't need to ask permission from his mother to go to the concert. Maybe other fifteen-year-olds' parents had rules and curfews and concerns for their kids. Not Greg's mom.

Greg doesn't remember much about that night. He was excited about Grace Slick and Jefferson Airplane. And he was amazed that he somehow ended up only about fifteen feet from the stage.

The band launched into "Somebody to Love" and the crowd went wild. People were screaming and pushing. Love beads were popping off everywhere as it started to get rough. It was hard to breathe. Greg couldn't see anything except his own feet and a blur of pushing arms and legs all around him.

A random person on the stage pulled him up onto it by his armpits. He bobbed and weaved around the sound equipment and got himself out of there. Much later, he discovered that the mayhem had actually been planned rather than spontaneous. Not very hippie-esque. Singer David Crosby had arranged for a pie fight while Jefferson Airplane was on the stage, and had about three hundred cream pies brought into the venue. While Greg was looking for rescue from the hippie scrum, he hadn't realized that all those people were in fact storming the stage not for somebody to love but for some pastries to throw.

Today, when pastor and evangelist Greg Laurie is preaching to a huge crowd in a stadium, he sometimes thinks about that crazy night when his determination to see Grace Slick almost ended in Piemaggedon. What if fifteen-year-old Greg Laurie could have somehow known that fifty years later *he'd* be the one on stage in a huge venue, and that the 161,000 people in the arena for a three-day event were there not to get stoned or to groove in a concert or to throw cream pies . . . but to hear the gospel, and that *he'd* be the one telling them about Jesus Christ?

That would have been far more bizarre to Greg than the freakiest, weirdest LSD trip he possibly could have taken back in 1968.

8

When Nitro Met Glycerin

Do not waste time bothering whether you "love" your neighbor; act as if you did.

C. S. Lewis

If we have got the true love of God shed abroad in our hearts, we will show it in our lives. We will not have to go up and down the earth proclaiming it. We will show it in everything we say or do.

Dwight L. Moody

In that convulsive year of 1968, Kay Smith was about forty years old. She had been a pastor's wife for almost half her life. She was a witty, intelligent, fun woman who was curious about everything and missed very little. She was a deep student of the Bible. She had shoulder-length black hair, bright blue eyes, and long, tapered fingers with oval fingernails. While Chuck Smith was a winsome, warm personality in the pulpit, he was quieter in a private setting. For her part,

Kay was inquisitive, verbal, and ebullient. She loved to talk with people and hear their stories.

In early 1968, though, Kay was moved by the stories of people she hadn't yet met.

Newspapers in Southern California were highlighting the influx of restless teenagers into the area. Many of them were runaways who'd rejected their parents' rules and materialistic values in favor of freedom and the open road. They'd come to San Francisco for the Summer of Love, but now it was cold in Northern California, so they'd made their way south to warmer cities. Young men and women were homeless and hitchhiking, easy prey for just about anyone. They'd go through trashcans looking for food, but somehow seemed to always have access to marijuana and harder drugs.

Kay made her husband drive over to Huntington Beach with her. It was a surfing beach about twenty minutes from their home. It was also home to the Golden Bear, a club that featured musicians like Jimi Hendrix and Janis Joplin. Huntington was a hippie magnet, with teenagers, peace signs, flowers, beads, and drugs everywhere. Kids wore buttons with the mantras of the day: "War is not healthy for children and other living things," "Save water, shower with a friend," and the seemingly omnipresent, "Make love, not war."

Chuck and Kay would watch kids staggering down the street or zoned out on the beach. Chuck would think practical, manly thoughts like, *Why don't you get a job and cut your hair and take a bath?*

Then he'd look over at his wife and she would have tears in her blue eyes. "They're so lost," Kay would say. "We've got to reach out to them! They've got to know a different life! They've got to know Jesus!"

Soon Chuck followed his wife's leading. Kay realized that if they waited for their paths to cross with one of these needy teenagers, it just wasn't going to happen. Lost hippies weren't going to spontaneously show up at their nice, conservative church one Sunday morning. They needed to do something.

Their college-age daughter was dating a guy who'd come to know Christ out of the Haight-Ashbury scene in San Francisco. So Kay asked the boyfriend if he could bring a real live hippie over to the Smiths' house. "We just want to understand their world," she said. "We want to know how they think, what they believe, and how we can help."

Soon after that, the Smiths' doorbell rang. Their daughter's boyfriend was standing on the porch along with a slender young man with long, brown hair, a mustache and beard, and a linen tunic. He had flowers in his hair and tiny, tinkling bells on his cuffs. He had a huge smile on his face.

"Come in!" said Kay.

"This is Lonnie," the boyfriend said. "Lonnie Frisbee. I was driving the other day, and I always try to pick up hippies who're hitchhiking so I can tell them about Jesus. So I picked up this guy here, and next thing I know, he's telling me that he hitchhikes around the area so he can tell the people who give him rides all about Jesus. He's our brother in Christ."

It was like when John Lennon met Paul McCartney, or Steve Jobs met Steve Wozniak. Or when nitro met glycerin. Explosive. Lonnie Frisbee and Chuck Smith were the same species; aside from that, they had nothing in common in terms of personality, life experience, background, or appearance. But they both knew Jesus, and when Lonnie crossed Chuck and Kay Smith's threshold, something big and volatile was about to happen that only God could orchestrate.

As they talked that evening, Chuck realized that Lonnie might be the very person God could use to help his church reach out to hippies, beach bums, and druggies. "You speak their language," he said to Lonnie. "You know better than any of us how, what, and why they think and feel the way they do. You could stay with us for a couple of weeks and help me understand what makes them tick."[1]

Lonnie was excited about the idea. "I could do that," he said. But, he added, he'd just gotten married to a girl who'd been caught up in the drug scene, like he had, but had left it all behind to follow Jesus. They were living in San Francisco.

"No problem," said Chuck. "Bring your wife. She can stay here too."

Soon Lonnie and his wife were living in the Smiths' home. But they had this irrepressible habit of reproducing . . . not physically but spiritually. They'd go out to the streets or the beach with fellow believers and talk to kids about Jesus Christ. Hippies would confess their sins, receive Jesus, and become sons and daughters of God. They'd leave their old lives behind. And some would move right in to the Smiths' home as well and be baptized in the backyard pool.

Chuck and Kay were called to many bold moves, but running a commune in their home was not one of them. Chuck rented out a house in Costa Mesa. The group moved in. They worked, shared meals and resources, and studied the Bible. They shared about Christ with other hippies. Within a few weeks there were thirty-five people living there. Chuck rented another house. The same thing happened. Eventually there were a half dozen new communities of young believers getting excited about Jesus and the Word of God.

Great as it is, the story of hippies coming to faith in Christ might have been just a blip on the religious radar if they had kept to themselves in their communes. What was of key importance, and what made the conversions of hippies in Costa Mesa not just a passing phenomenon but an enduring movement of the Holy Spirit, was the fact that many of these kids came right into the local church.

Chuck Smith's church, to be exact.

Chuck's church was not perfect. It was full of imperfect people, just like the first-century church in the book of Acts. Back then the church was called the *ekklesia* in the Greek, the visible gathering of believers. The word is used 114 times in the New Testament, and at least ninety of those times it refers to specific, local groups of Christ followers. The book of Acts shows God's people coming together in local churches that are devoted to God's Word, to fellowship with one another, to worship, and to prayer.[2]

The local church—humble as it is, filled with flawed but redeemed human beings—is God's ordained instrument for spreading His good news to people of every tribe and nation. Whether today or fifty years ago, the strength or weakness of any movements, parachurch ministries, or people depends largely on their connection to the local church. The stronger the connection, the greater and longer the impact of that movement in its lasting influence on the culture. The weaker the connection, the weaker the impact.

What gave legs to the Jesus Movement as it happened in Southern California—specifically in Orange County, and later in Riverside, Downey, West Covina, San Diego, and elsewhere—was its connection to local churches.

It was a Wednesday evening service in Chuck Smith's little *ekklesia* in Costa Mesa, circa 1968. Chuck had just prayed the customary opening prayer, and his congregation of businessmen, moms, dads, and other upstanding citizens looked up, waiting for his sermon.

Then, in the silence, came the small but distinct sound of bells. Little bells tinkling on the ankles of about fifteen hippies who were wearing granny dresses, jeans, cutoffs, tie-dye shirts, headbands, and flowers in their long hair. They walked down the aisle. Most had never set their bare feet inside a church before. They looked at the pews but chose to move all the way to the front, where they sat down cross-legged on the floor right in front of the pulpit, waiting expectantly to hear whatever it was that Pastor Chuck Smith had to say.

There was a collective gasp from the pews, then silence in Calvary Chapel. Chuck looked at his congregation. His congregation looked at the hippies. The hippies smiled back, holding their new Bibles in their laps.

"Well," said Chuck heartily. "Tonight we're continuing our series in the letters of the apostle John. So let's all open our Bibles to the book of 1 John!" Chuck read:

Dear friends, let us love one another, for love comes from God. Everyone who loves has been born of God and knows God. Whoever does not love does not know God, because God is love. This is how God showed his love among us: He sent his one and only Son into the world that we might live through him. This is love: not that we loved God, but that he loved us and sent his Son as an atoning sacrifice for our sins. Dear friends, since God so loved us, we also ought to love one another.[3]

So it was not a campaign or an outreach or a program or a human plan that kicked off the Jesus Revolution in Costa Mesa in 1968. It was, like all awakenings or revivals, initiated by the Spirit of God. The Holy Spirit opened Kay Smith's heart to people who were on the margins of society, people who weren't like her. The Spirit—who clearly has a sense of humor—linked two such unlikely brothers as Chuck Smith and Lonnie Frisbee. And the Spirit drew hippies and conservative church people together into an unlikely new community, one built not by human plans or preferences but by the revolutionary love of God.

9

Meanwhile, in Malaysia

There is no pit so deep, that God's love is not deeper still.

Corrie ten Boom

Six thousand miles from Newport Beach, California, the flower children's pollen wafted into the Kuala Lumpur home of a twelve-year-old girl named Cathe Martin. Cathe's dad, Dick, was a marketing analysis manager with Esso, the oil company that eventually became Exxon. The Martins enjoyed a comfortable life with servants, nannies, and a chauffeur in their expat neighborhood within the capital of Malaysia.

Cathe's mother, Pilar, was Spanish. She was deeply and passionately Catholic, while Cathe's father was fairly reserved about expressing anything personal, from his feelings to his religious views.

Cathe was a sensitive girl with a mystical bent. As a six-year-old, she saw the then-famous movie *Spartacus* with actor Kirk Douglas in the title role. She had nightmares for years about the crucifixion scene. She was fascinated by the stories of saints, and loved to look at brightly colored prayer cards depicting the life of Saint Teresa of the Little Flower, or Saint Bernadette's mystical vision of the Blessed Virgin at a grotto in Lourdes.

Cathe loved the long, lace veils that her mother and other ladies wore to mass. She loved the candles and the smell of incense; it all seemed so beautiful and holy. The nuns had told her that seven years old was the age of accountability; at six, Cathe thought, *Good, I've got one more year until I'm held responsible for my sins.*

Shortly after reaching that point, she went to the priest to make her confession. She slipped into the little confessional booth and sat down. Her feet barely touched the ground. On the other side of the wooden divider in the cubicle, the priest waited.

"Bless me, Father, for I have sinned," Cathe began.

"Yes, my child?" said the priest.

But the sin on Cathe's seven-year-old heart was too gross, too dark, and too terrible to tell. She couldn't do it. So she quickly made something else up, something she actually *could* confess to the unseen priest on the other side of the divide.

"I, uh . . . I kicked my maid!"

From these and other experiences, Cathe took away two main impressions from the faith of her childhood. First, God was Other. He was far away, remote, mysterious, and inapproachable. And second, she carried a dark, vague burden of guilt.

Cathe's two older sisters, Mary and Dodie, had been in school in the Philippines and in Switzerland during the previous school year, but they both came home for the summer of 1967. Dodie was fifteen and Mary was eighteen.

Cathe was a sensitive younger sister, and all she could see was that her sisters didn't hang out at the dinner table; they didn't want to go out and ride bikes or go bowling or have fun. They just wanted to sit in their rooms, listening to Led Zeppelin, Jimi Hendrix, Janis Joplin, and the Beatles. They no longer wore cute little cotton dresses with perky accessories. Their hair wasn't perfect anymore. Instead, it was long skirts, torn jeans, flowing shirts, and wild, long hair that didn't even look brushed. They constantly talked back to their parents, slammed doors, and yelled.

Cathe would creep into their bedrooms at night. "What's going on?" she'd ask. "What happened to you guys at school last semester?"

They told her how their friends had started smoking dope and how they'd gotten into it too. Cathe had never heard of marijuana. But, as she was soon to find out, it was easy to get in Kuala Lumpur. Mary was dating a guy who was a little bit older, and he had shown her where to go in the city to buy packets of really good ganja.

"It's so cool," Mary told Cathe. "I can't explain. It's like you listen to music and you really get it, or you rub your fingers over the surface of the car and it's soooooooooo smooth. Or food! It just tastes so good. Everything's more colorful, more mellow, you feel the texture, you just *feel* more!"

Drug use wasn't new in Kuala Lumpur. Opium abuse had been a reality among older Chinese men in Malaysia for a century. In the mid-1960s, authorities tolerated it, as they assumed that the deaths of this older generation would mean the end of Malaysia's drug problems. But with the growing hippie culture and drug habits of American soldiers on leave for R & R in Malaysia, marijuana, heroin, and psychedelic drug use skyrocketed, and the authorities would soon crack down.

As that Malaysian summer rolled on, Cathe got more and more into the new world her sisters were telling her about. Some of it seemed sketchy; she didn't think much of her sister playing strip poker with the guys who lived next door. But Cathe had always been artistic and reflective, and this artsy new world sounded so much more interesting than the squared-off corners of Catholic school and a lifetime of rules.

Cathe's parents were not quite as fascinated by Mary and Dodie's new preoccupations. They got more and more worried, as Mary not only smoked lots of dope but also moved on to uppers, downers, and other pills.

One night the teenaged guy next door, who'd been smoking opium, slipped Mary some barbiturates. Next thing Cathe knew, her family was sitting at the dinner table and Mary was acting strangely. She'd start a sentence and then leave it hanging in midair. Food was falling off her fork. The tension between Mary and her father started to escalate. They began to shout at each other. Dodie, age fifteen, was trying to intervene. "Come on, guys," she kept saying. "Just chill out!"

They weren't going to chill out. Mary stood up, spewing profanities and knocking her chair backwards. Dick stood up, furious. He slapped Mary across the face.

"Go ahead, do it again!" she shrieked. He did.

Cathe had never, ever seen her dad lose control in such a way.

Mary ran upstairs to her room, slammed the door, and took even more pills. Peacekeeper Dodie ran out the front door, crying. Dick and Pilar ran out after her.

They brought Dodie back in, but by now Mary had fled out the back door.

The Martins lived in a nice subdivision, but it was surrounded by thick jungle full of snakes, animals, and who knows what. Especially in her altered state, Mary wasn't safe out there. Cathe's parents went back out in the night. They were gone for hours. Cathe cowered in her bed, and finally her mom and dad came home, holding on to Mary. They brewed a big pot of strong black coffee and walked their daughter up and down the halls of the house.

In spite of the drama, Cathe had bought in to the hippie vibe by the end of the summer. There was something about the rebellion that was intoxicating. And on a far more superficial level—after all, she was twelve—she loved the clothes. She loved the idea of wearing a vintage tuxedo jacket with a long, flowing skirt. And she loved the fact that perfectly straight, precisely parted hair was no longer the thing. Cathe had always had curly, rebellious tresses; now her hair was just right. In the same way, her slim figure was cool too. She didn't have to be a Barbie doll; part of being a hippie was just being yourself. Natural, not plastic.

Like parents of wandering teenagers everywhere, Cathe's parents were beside themselves with concern. Pilar responded verbally. First, she talked and talked and talked to her girls, cautioning them about the dangers of the choices they were making. "You're hurting your father," she would say. "You're going to end up in an alley with a needle in your arm!"

The girls loved their parents, but they were just not in a place where dire warnings made sense. They wanted to live free, maybe move to a commune and share organic food, getting high and strumming guitars; everything was mellow.

The only problems in their lives, really, were adults who tried to make them feel guilty.

Cathe's mom also enlisted spiritual help from the big guns. Pilar went to the Carmelite nuns and told them her troubles. They prayed for Cathe and her sisters but also told Pilar, "Don't worry! Worry is a sin! Just pray!"

Easy for them to say, Pilar thought. *They're not mothers!* But she did her best to follow their advice, and she constantly went to church, lighting candles and praying for her wandering daughters.

Cathe's dad didn't consult the nuns. He looked for a geographical cure and decided to make a dramatic change. Esso had a new job for him back in the US, in New Jersey. But Pilar hated cold weather. So Dick opted to leave Esso altogether and to start up a new business as a financial planner. Together, the Martins decided to get their family out of Southeast Asia to a safer environment, one that was far from the allure of the hippie lifestyle.

Ironically, they settled in Southern California. Not exactly a hippie-free zone.

10

Magnificent Desolation

> The caged bird sings with a fearful trill,
> of things unknown, but longed for still,
> and his tune is heard on the distant hill,
> for the caged bird sings of freedom.
>
> Maya Angelou,
> "I Know Why the Caged Bird Sings"

No one could have predicted the paradoxes, ironies, explosions, and potentials of the last year of the 1960s. For individual young people like Greg Laurie, as well as for many in the nation as a whole, the world felt like a ball of confusion.

At the beginning of the 1960s, the golden young president had looked ahead with great hope. In speeches before a joint session of Congress and at Rice University, President Kennedy called on the United States to commit itself to achieving the goal of landing a man on the moon before the end of the decade. Kennedy believed that space itself could be a "theater of peace" rather than a force for ill, but only if the

US achieved preeminence in the space race with the Soviet Union.[1]

John Kennedy never got to see his Americans on the moon. By 1969 both he and his brother Robert were gone, shot down by assassins. The decade that had started with high hopes for cosmic peace and exploration was ending in violence, war, and social unrest.

Still, on July 20, 1969, there was one moment that brought the entire nation together, almost like those sunnier days of the 1950s, around the television set. Six hundred million people tuned in to watch, in living color, as Americans landed on the moon.

First, astronaut Neil Armstrong slowly descended the space ladder from his silver rocket ship. He planted his bulky, booted feet on the powdery surface of the moon.

Armstrong's giant leap for mankind was followed about twenty minutes later by his fellow astronaut Buzz Aldrin's stroll on the lunar surface. (Buzz also became the first human to urinate while on the moon, but that's another story.) By now Kennedy's nemesis, that scowly Richard Nixon, was president. He called from the White House to congratulate the astronauts. Viewers were absolutely boondoggled, not just by the technology of the lunar landing itself but by the fact that the president of the United States could somehow chat on the phone with two guys hanging out 239,000 miles away.

Neil Armstrong's words in the midst of his historic moment are well-known. Buzz Aldrin's thoughts about his walk on the moon are both less familiar and more poignant. The first phrase that came to his mind, he said later, was "magnificent desolation." He thought about the "magnificence of human beings . . . Planet Earth, maturing the technologies, imagination and courage to . . . dream about being on the Moon, and then . . . carrying out that dream—achieving that is a magnificent testimony to humanity.

"But it is also desolate," Aldrin continued. "There is no place on earth as desolate as what I was viewing in those first moments on the Lunar Surface. . . . I realized what I was looking at, towards the horizon in every direction, had not changed in hundreds, thousands of years . . . no atmosphere, black sky.

"Cold. Colder than anyone could experience on Earth. . . . No sign of life whatsoever. . . . More desolate than any place on Earth."[2]

In some ways, Aldrin's "magnificent desolation" could serve as a tagline for the decade.

Magnificence, '60s-style, included the best and the brightest scientists achieving the extraordinary goal of President Kennedy's glorious dream for Americans to arrive on the moon. There was also the magnificence of the persevering courage of the civil rights movement, and the high hopes of the hippies and others who were searching for peace, love, and understanding. Many of the younger generation earnestly rejected the staid material values of their parents' era, seeking brighter colors of community, meaning, creativity, and new horizons.

But there was desolation as well. At the beginning of the decade, the best and brightest minds in political leadership had pursued a policy that led to tens of thousands of young American men being brutally killed in a faraway war. Those who made it home were spit on in the streets. Many hippies—those "gentle people" with flowers in their hair—who had pursued a brightly colored revolution of freedom, found themselves as confined as their parents, trapped in addictions, destructive relationships, discord, and disappointment. The sweet life of the commune, contentedly nibbling brown rice, had become dumpster diving for half-eaten trash on dirty streets. The "harmony and understanding" and "mystic crystal revelation" of the Age of Aquarius turned out to be a fleeting experience, not an ongoing and dependable reality.

For many, the '60s were a wild ride. Some might call it magnificent. But most didn't end up at the destination they had hoped for. Sex, drugs, and rock and roll could only roll so far, and sometimes the ride ended at a pretty desolate place.

In mid-August 1969, half a million young people gathered at a New York dairy farm for what many consider the last great hoorah of the hippie movement: Woodstock. Thirty-two great bands. Rain. Mud. Drugs. Peaceful youth getting "back to the garden." It would become a cultural touchstone, a time of stardust, golden magic that flickered for four days in the rain and then faded away.

Kurt Vonnegut, author of 1969's blockbuster novel *Slaughterhouse Five* and hero of the antiwar movement, later said of Woodstock on a PBS panel discussion, "I think it represents a very primitive need in all of us. . . . At our peril we do without a tribe, without a support system. The nuclear family is not a support system. It's hideously vulnerable. And so we again and again join gangs."[3]

Vonnegut's interviewer called Woodstock "an extended family," a community, and a support system.[4]

Another member of the PBS panel noted the dark side to all this "very thin idea of community." The legitimate hunger for family had led some to a hideous counterfeit. "Just a few days before Woodstock, it's worth remembering 'the family' that murdered Sharon Tate, and that Charlie Manson was a version of what could come out of this kind of pseudo-tribalism in a drug-addled atmosphere."[5]

He was referring to the gruesome headlines that had splashed across the front pages of newspapers around the whole country the week before Woodstock. Charles Manson, the ex-con drifter who had built his commune of lost young women, the Manson "Family," commissioned two nights of murder in Los Angeles. A group of his followers had already killed and dismembered several hangers-on unlucky enough to cross their path. And on August 9, 1969, they slaughtered actress Sharon Tate and four of her friends. The next night they butchered a middle-aged couple in their LA home.

Manson saw an apocalyptic war coming between the races. He called it "Helter Skelter," and his disciples scrawled that phrase on a wall in their victims' blood. Manson had fused everything bad about the times and the darkness in his own heart into a bloody tide of mayhem. His followers were fresh-faced teenaged girls who'd run away from home to the communal security of Charlie's family. They slept with Charlie, cooked for Charlie, carved Xs on their foreheads for Charlie, and killed for Charlie. They giggled in the courtroom during their eventual trial.

Unlike Woodstock, the Manson Family represented the darkest extreme of a few in the hippie movement.

Then, though it was billed by some as a West Coast Woodstock, the Altamont Speedway music festival on December 6, 1969, became an icon for the dark side of the countercultural movement. Santana, Jefferson Airplane, the Flying Burrito

Brothers, Crosby, Stills, Nash & Young, and the Grateful Dead were on the lineup; the Rolling Stones were to take the stage for the finale.

But the evening began to deteriorate. Perhaps this had something to do with the fact that the Hells Angels, who'd been hired as security for $500 worth of beer, were getting more violent with every beer they downed. Feeling the bad vibe, the Dead declined to play.

The crowd got violent too. Fights broke out. One performer, who was six months pregnant, was hit in the head by a beer bottle that fractured her skull. The Hells Angels were pushing people back from the stage with sawed-off pool cues and motorcycle chains. Marty Balin of Jefferson Airplane was punched in the head and knocked unconscious.

By the time Mick Jagger finally took the stage, he'd already been hit in the head by an attendee. During the Stones' third song, "Sympathy for the Devil," an eighteen-year-old fan named Meredith Hunter tried to get on stage. He was repelled by security. High on methamphetamines, he left and returned later in the set with a gun, which he pulled from his jacket. One of the Hells Angels pulled a knife from his belt and stabbed Hunter repeatedly. (A jury later ruled that the Angel acted in self-defense.) The teenager died on the ground in front of the stage.

After it was all over, there was only the wreckage. Trash, human waste, dozens of people injured, extensive property damage, and lots of stolen cars and drugs. Three other people besides Meredith Hunter died that night. Two were victims of a hit-and-run accident, and one drowned in an irrigation canal near the venue.

Later—much later—the *New Yorker* concluded that Altamont ended a utopian dream, "the idea that, left to their own inclinations and stripped of the trappings of the wider social order, the young people of the new generation will somehow spontaneously create a higher, gentler, more loving grassroots order. What died at Altamont is [that] . . . dream itself."[6]

That last big concert of the '60s became a symbol of all that had gone dark in a decade that had promised such bright colors. The flower power, the love beads, the innocence of psychedelic dreams . . . it all ended in shades of gray, with sympathy for the devil, knives and guns and violence. To this day, the unforgettable film footage shot that night—the snuffing of a human being in the *Gimme Shelter* documentary— looks a lot like people making war, not love.

"They said Altamont was the end of an era," Jefferson Airplane's Grace Slick said later, "which more or less is true. It coincided with the way things rise and fall. Everything does that. Look at the Roman Empire. Sometimes it takes two years, sometimes it takes 500. Everything is born, rises and then dies."[7]

To cap off Grace Slick's perspective, it's worth quoting the Woodstock Preservation Alliance's analysis of the end of the era:

The year preceding [Woodstock] had been of one of the most violent in post-World War II history. The long struggle for African-American civil rights had been forestalled following the assassination of its most articulate leader, the Reverend Martin Luther King, Jr. His murder had provoked rioting and arson in most of the nation's largest cities. . . . Protests against American involvement in Vietnam had drawn thousands of people into the streets, most notably in Chicago the previous summer at the Democratic National Convention. . . . A growing perception among women of their own lack of social and economic equality prompted the emergence of a new wave of feminism . . . Women's Liberation. College campuses were convulsed with sit-ins opposing the Vietnam War. . . . During the month before the Festival a routine police raid on a gay bar in Greenwich Village touched off the Stonewall riots, which itself marked the birth of the Gay and Lesbian Liberation movement.

All of these crises and disruptions to the status quo produced a feeling among many Americans, and particularly the youth, that the country was coming unraveled. Among the more radical segment of political and cultural activists on the left there was an increasing sense that *the next American revolution might be at hand.*[8]

Interesting: "The next American revolution might be at hand"?

And so it was.

11

The Long and Winding Road

It is God to whom and with whom we travel,
and while He is the end of our journey,
He is also at every stopping place.

Elisabeth Elliot

Greg Laurie's personal Jesus Revolution may well have started with the prayers of Kay Smith.

Kay and Chuck Smith's neat, one-story bungalow was in a modest neighborhood just a few blocks from Newport Beach's Harbor High School.

Sometimes, in the afternoons, Kay would look out her sparkling, Windexed living room window and see kids ambling home from school. She'd see high school boys with their long hair and the rolling walk of people who've been smoking dope. Sometimes she could hear scraps of inane conversation. Kay's heart went out to them with the same compassion she'd felt when she'd first seen the hippies in Huntington Beach. So she'd stop whatever she was doing, right there in her living room, and pray for the kids on the street. She didn't know, of course, that the one with the long, blond hair and the art papers stuck under his arm was a lost, high seventeen-year-old named Greg Laurie.

Greg didn't feel like he was seventeen. To put it in the words of the Beatles' song, he felt like he'd already been down a very long and winding road—and, sadly, it hadn't led to anyone's door. He'd been beaten, mocked, or ignored by his mother's not-so-significant others when he was little. His mom had sent him off to military school. Because of her serial husbands, he'd gone to way too many schools and moved way too many times. He'd refined his artistic skills sitting in bars at night, drawing cartoons while he waited for his mom to nightcap off her evening. He had heroes—cartoonists like Charles Schultz, the creator of *Peanuts*, for example. But his everyday experience was that the adults he actually knew were just the people who let you down, broke their word, or sent you to the principal's office. He dreamed of great things, of one day being in a place where everybody knew his name. But he had no idea how to get there.

Greg had thought that drugs might be the ticket for that journey. But all he'd found was that they were not exactly a path to cosmic creativity and celestial self-discovery. LSD promised psychedelic colors and a rainbow of higher consciousness, but all it did for Greg was take him to dark, bleak places where he saw his face melting and all that was left was a skull. Acid had permanently cracked some kids he knew; they downed it like candy, and now they'd never be the same. Pot was not much better; it dulled him out and leached his creativity. He'd think he'd drawn something extraordinary, only to look at it the next day and realize that all he'd sketched was a million mushrooms and marijuana leaves, like wallpaper for a hippie bathroom.

He'd seen Jesus freaks on the street; they'd hand him tracts when he'd go down to the pier to score some pot. The tracts didn't make any sense, really, but he'd kept them stuffed in a "God drawer" in his room, like a raccoon saving treasures he didn't quite understand.

He'd read a book called *Sun Signs*, the first astrology book to ever get a spot on the *New York Times* bestseller list. Among other things, it told him that as a Sagittarius, he was full of "idealistic enthusiasm and curiosity." Because of his "sunny optimism," there would almost always be a crowd around him. He was so optimistic, in fact, that "if his enemies mailed him a huge carton of manure, he wouldn't be offended. He'd just figure they forgot to include the horse."[1]

Bottom line, the book itself sounded a bit like a carton of manure.

Greg wasn't a huge Rolling Stones fan, but the fact was, he couldn't get no satisfaction. Drugs, sex, music, alcohol, school, and the adult world all had been tried and found wanting. Life looked like a long spool, most of it as yet unwound, but there sure didn't seem to be any promise that the future would be any different from the past.

It was a sunny, mid-March day in 1970. He was on his way to go off campus to buy some drugs.

A week or so earlier, a total eclipse of the sun had turned the day into darkness across much of the United States.

In New York, members of the Weather Underground—a radical leftist group opposed to the Vietnam War—died when the bomb they were assembling to blow up a US Army base exploded prematurely in their Greenwich Village townhouse.

The United States lowered the national voting age from twenty-one to eighteen.

An Eastern Air Lines flight from Newark to Boston was hijacked by a guy armed with a .38-caliber revolver. After a gun battle in the cockpit, the pilot was somehow able to land the plane safely.

Simon and Garfunkel's "Bridge Over Troubled Water" was the number one song in America. The Beatles released a new album, *Let It Be*.

The US military announced its five hundredth nuclear test explosion since 1945.

At Harbor High School, however, Greg Laurie wasn't thinking much about the national news of the day. Nor was he pondering the rise and fall of great civilizations, or the hippie movement, or much of anything. He was pondering how to sneak off campus to smoke pot and checking out what cute girls were doing.

There was one girl in particular. Her magnetism didn't have to do with being attractive, however. Greg was drawn to her because she seemed so happy and free.

There was one big problem, though. At school, she carried around a Bible the size of an atlas, and she was clearly a Jesus freak.

During lunch hour on that fine March day in 1970, this girl was sitting in the grass with about thirty other students, singing folk songs to one kid's guitar, and smiling way too much. Greg inched just close enough to see what they were doing, but not close enough to seem like he was part of the group. As always, he was an observer.

The singing was pretty plain, but it also seemed pure. As a cynic, Greg could sniff out insincerity, and these kids were actually, really into Jesus. *There's Bill up there singing*, he thought. *And I used to get stoned with him. Now, it's like he really is different.*

Then, as the music faded, a guy got up. And he looked just like . . . Jesus. He wasn't quite the pale Jesus portrait on Greg's grandparents' living room wall, but pretty close. He had long, dark hair parted in the middle, with a mustache and beard. He had peaceful brown eyes. He was wearing sandals and a flowing shirt that looked like a first-century tunic.

Greg didn't know the guy's name then, but it was Lonnie Frisbee. As he continued to evangelize throughout the Costa Mesa area, Lonnie had come to Greg's public high school to teach a Bible study during lunchtime.

Lonnie read out loud from the Bible and talked about how Jesus wasn't some faraway, dry historical figure. He was real, and human beings at Harbor High School in 1970 could actually have a relationship with Him.

Greg thought Jesus was great; he'd seen all His movies, like *Ben Hur* and *King of Kings*. He knew that Jesus was a good teacher who probably would have fit right in with all the peace-loving hippies of the day.

Lonnie talked about how Jesus was the Son of God, that He had died for everyone's sins, and that He had risen from the dead. For the first time in his life, Greg made a personal connection. He realized that Jesus had died for *his* sins, and that Jesus was alive and speaking to Greg through this hippie evangelist.

Then Lonnie said something that forced the point: "Jesus said that 'You're either for Me, or you're against Me.'

"There's no middle ground with Jesus," Lonnie went on. "You're either for Him or against Him. So which side are you on?"

Whoa, Greg thought. Jesus wasn't just part of the nice hippie blur of peace and love and harmony, take some of what He said if you like it, skip the other parts you don't like so much, make Him part of your own little world. He was actually more radical than that. More revolutionary: you were either for Him or against Him.

Greg looked at the Jesus-freak kids sitting there with their Bibles on their laps. They'd clearly made a decision. It was actually cool that they didn't seem to care what other people thought. They were for Jesus.

I'm not part of them, Greg thought. *So does that mean I'm against Jesus?*

Lonnie Frisbee went on. Anyone who wanted to decide to be for Jesus could come forward and he would pray with them.

It was scary. Greg thought, *What if it's not real? What if I can't do it right? What if it works for everybody else but me?*

But in the end, all he knew was he wanted to be for Jesus, not against Him. His body somehow made its way up to the front toward Lonnie, the Jesus lookalike, along with other students who'd decided the same thing. They all stood there. Quiet.

Then, after some earnest words of simple instruction from Lonnie, Greg prayed to tell Jesus that he was for Him, that he wanted to follow Him, and that he wanted Jesus to forgive his sins.

All the other kids erupted into tears and hugs. Greg just stood there. He felt nothing except the sneaking suspicion that he just hadn't done it right. But then he felt something else. It was the sense that a weight had been lifted, a burden he hadn't even consciously known he had carried all his life. His long and winding road had, in fact, led to the Door.

12

The Adult in the Room

Everybody can be great, because everybody can serve. You
don't have to have a college degree to serve. You don't have
to make your subject and your verb agree to serve. . . . You
only need a heart full of grace, a soul generated by love.

Martin Luther King Jr.

Like many brand-new believers at the time, Greg never got
the memo that continuing to use drugs was probably not a
good idea. A few days after his conversion, he was wondering
if anything spiritual had really happened to him. He went
with some friends to a canyon to smoke dope. It was like
a hundred other times; he would think great thoughts and
realize later that they were nothing. But life as usual, dull as
it was, seemed like it might be preferable to the strange new
world of being a Jesus person.

But then a strange thing happened. For no apparent reason, the pot had no appeal. It seemed pitiful, like a cheap

substitute for something he really wanted. He didn't need it anymore.

Greg pitched his pipe, and his dope, as far as he could into the woods.

It wasn't as if a preacher had jumped out from behind a tree and confronted Greg about the perils of reefer madness. It was that same low-key but sure nudge that he had felt at Harbor High School. Something was different about him now.

A day or two after that, he went to his first church service. He hadn't been to any church except with his grandparents when he was young. He had dim memories of long hymns, longer sermons, and lots of old people in sparsely filled pews.

When he got to Calvary Chapel in Costa Mesa, the parking lot was full of cars. Most of them had bumper stickers with cheerful messages like "Have a nice eternity!" and "Things go better with Christ!" Inside, the sanctuary was as packed as the parking lot. Most of the people had big, fat Bibles; they were teenagers and hippies and businessmen and moms and kids and everybody in between. They filled the seats, the aisles, and the extra chairs that had been set up.

An older guy came up the aisle toward Greg. He was an usher, but Greg didn't know what a church usher even was.

"Welcome, brother!" the man said. "I can find a seat for you." He took Greg all the way up to the front, where he could squeeze in on the first row.

Not good, Greg thought. *No way to escape.*

The music was like he'd heard at the little Bible study on his high school campus. Simple, but strong and pure, and everyone was singing their hearts out. People were putting their arms around each other, hugging, and some had tears in their eyes. The guy and the girl on either side of him put their arms around his shoulders, called him "brother," and welcomed him in.

Greg had never seen anything like it. He'd come from a home where his mother had never, ever sincerely told him that she loved him. She never hugged or embraced him in any way. He'd protected himself for as long as he could remember with a shell of cynicism. He never hugged anyone. And he could smell fakers, users, and liars in a moment.

But here, there was nothing but a huge tide of love from all these people who accepted him, and each other, sincerely. It was real. It was terrifying. It felt absolutely wonderful.

But all good things must come to an end. Eventually the beautiful worship music was over, and then a bald guy with a big smile came out with a Bible.

Oh no, thought Greg. *Here comes the adult.*

For him, adults were the people he got in trouble with in the principal's office, or the staff at his military school when he was young, or the flashy men who hung around his mom in bars. Adults were not to be trusted.

Chuck Smith sat down on a stool and began to talk. He was energetic but not theatrical. He spoke in an easy baritone voice in clear, understandable terms, not confusing religious language. He made sense. He seemed like a doctor, or maybe an airplane pilot or a favorite uncle: someone who was in charge, someone you could trust. And when he talked about Jesus, Greg felt more and more intrigued. This was what he wanted. This was what he'd been looking for without even knowing it. He wanted to learn and really understand about Jesus. He had a feeling that everything else would fall into place after that.

After that first worship service, Greg began to get the hang of his strange and wonderful new life. He couldn't wait to go to church, and fortunately for him, there were services there four nights a week. On other nights there were Bible studies or opportunities to get together with new friends and go out to tell people about Jesus.

He didn't want to dabble with the dark side anymore. Drugs, sex, foul language, cutting other people down . . . it was actually a relief to let go of the things that now had no appeal. Growing up as he had, he had seen enough of "the world" for a lifetime. When church kids would cuss at school in order to seem cool around non-Christians, or experiment with drugs or alcohol, he wanted to hit them upside the head. *That stuff is absolutely dead*, he'd think. *Why are they even messing around with it?*

It's worth noting that Greg would think the same thing almost fifty years later, wondering why some contemporary pastors, perhaps in an effort to appear culturally relevant, would brag about knocking back shots with celebrities, or cuss while giving a sermon, or engage in behaviors that, if not dangerous to them, might well cause others to stray. Greg wasn't puritanical about alcohol or cussing; he just felt like they didn't do a whole lot to honor God, and their negative effects far outweighed any potentially positive justifications.

Seventeen-year-old Greg felt a great sense of acceptance and unity at Calvary Chapel. He didn't realize then that it had not come naturally to many of the longtime attendees of the church. When hippies and long-haired kids had first arrived, the older people hadn't felt a natural sense of acceptance, and Chuck Smith had to shepherd them from their cultural preferences to biblical thinking. "The 'straight society,'" Chuck said later, meaning "those from traditional backgrounds, simply found these excited young believers too far outside the norm to be welcomed with open arms and hearts."[1]

Chuck's traditional churchgoers expected conformity, respectability, cleanliness, and decency. They saw kids wearing everything from Native American tribal headgear to hippie accessories that clearly had come from a folk planet in outer space. The adults felt threatened. They worried that their own squeaky-clean Sunday school kids would fall under the influence of the counterculturists. Some equated differences in style with character deficiencies, and concluded the hippies were therefore freeloaders who needed to change their clothes and change their attitudes.

As is usually the case in churches, the dissension came from just a few individuals who fanned the flames. One such man's attitude changed after a Saturday when a group was working together to rehab the old school building on Calvary's property. To his surprise, the hippies worked hard, sweating in the summer sun as they pulled old tiles off the roof. By the end of the day, some of them had blistered, bleeding hands, but they just kept on working, singing choruses and joking together.

The church member realized that, yes, someone needed to change. *Him.* Something hard in his heart melted, and from that evening onward, he became one of the most ardent defenders of the hippie Christians.

Another skeptic, a well-known surgeon in the area, did not hide his disdain very well when he found himself sharing a packed pew with hippies one Sunday morning. He spent the opening hymns alternately checking his watch and staring in derision at the long-haired young man next to him. He could not wait for the church service to be over. Then it was time for the congregation to stand and read a Bible passage out loud. The surgeon did not have a Bible with him. The shaggy hippie nudged him and handed the surgeon his worn, well-read Bible. The surgeon gingerly took the Bible like it was full of infectious disease.

But then he saw that the pages were marked with handwritten notes and color highlighters. There was underlining everywhere, and exclamation points. This Bible was well-loved . . . and the surgeon felt the conviction of the Holy Spirit as he thought of his own hygienic but unmarked Bible at home on the bookshelf. *I'm the one who is wrong*, he thought. *I am sorry!*

As those crucial early weeks of cultural collision continued, the Holy Spirit worked on the church people's hearts, and so did Chuck Smith. He called a meeting. "I don't want it said that we preach an easy Christian experience at Calvary Chapel," he told his flock,

> but neither do I want to see us fall into the mistakes made by [churches] 30 years ago. They unintentionally drove out and therefore lost an entire generation of young people with their philosophies: no movies, no dancing, no smoking, etc. Their brand of gospel yielded disastrous results. We won't make this mistake at Calvary. We will instead trust God and place the emphasis on the work being accomplished in individuals by the Holy Spirit. This approach is both exciting and natural if the Spirit is given the opportunity to direct change in people. We need to avoid demanding conformance to a Western Christian lifestyle of short hair, clean-shaven, appropriate dress. The change will occur from the inside out.[2]

Chuck Smith's understanding of cultural Christianity was the key to Calvary Chapel's Jesus Revolution. Today's version of cultural Christianity is different. The things that shocked nice, churchgoing Christians in 1970 now seem tame. But the point is the same. Whether church members flinch at outer appearances like long hair or hippie dress or tattoos or any form of clothing, they need to take care to discern their own inner habits of the heart that might be less overt and more conventionally acceptable. The pursuit of money. Career success. Prestige or popularity. Passions like prejudice, drugs, food, drink . . . today, as in 1970, idols come in all forms, and they must fall before God Himself. If Christianity takes on the subtle values of the culture around it and adopts these as forms of faith, then there is no Jesus Revolution. Just religion. And religion cannot change or liberate any human soul. It just imposes a new form of slavery.

13

Jesus Music

In the divine Scriptures, there are shallows and there are deeps; shallows where the lamb may wade, and deeps where the elephant may swim.

John Owen, Puritan preacher

During those early days of Greg's experience of the Jesus Revolution, it would be hard to overestimate Lonnie Frisbee's influence on Calvary Chapel. Chuck Smith conducted services on Monday nights, and Lonnie would do so on Wednesday nights. The combination of their skills and gifts was always explosive in terms of the church's growth, but you could be certain that most of the drama would transpire on Wednesday nights. It was surprising: even though Lonnie had the gravitas of looking just like everybody's mental picture of Jesus, he was a slender, physically unimposing person who didn't read well and often mispronounced words. But Lonnie had a power that was more than the sum of his parts.

When he spoke or taught, kids would stand up all over the packed chapel to receive Christ.

Then, after the chapel services, Lonnie would have follow-up "afterglow" meetings in a side room. He'd dim the lights and preside over extended times of singing and prayer. Then he'd begin to call things out about kids who were in the room.

"There's someone in here who has a problem with his neck," he'd say from the front. People would be standing, swaying, and then someone would say, "Yes! That's me!" That person would come to the front, Lonnie would pray for him or her, and usually the hurting person would swoon to the floor. People were lined up in a row to catch those who fell.

For Greg, this was all new, just like the experience of even being in church was new. He noticed that if Chuck Smith was around, Lonnie was more reined in. But if Chuck wasn't there, Lonnie would focus more on getting people to pray in unintelligible languages or to fall down in the front of the church. Lonnie told him it was called "being slain in the Spirit."

Greg reasoned that God could, of course, do anything He wanted. Ever the observer, though, he also saw that people could get a bit hooked on emotions and psychological suggestions, looking for a certain thrilling experience over and over. He felt more centered when Chuck was in charge, teaching everybody straight from the Bible.

Still, Greg saw Lonnie as a role model.

He grew his hair out like Lonnie's. He dressed like Lonnie. He was flattered one afternoon when Lonnie asked him to help him get ready for a Bible study later that evening.

They went to Lonnie's small house. Creeping Charlie plants and Boston ferns overflowed from hand-glazed pots suspended in macramé hangers. The walls were covered with Lonnie's oil paintings of historic California missions. Other large canvases leaned against the back of an old green sofa.

Lonnie changed out of his T-shirt and put on one of his Jesus tunics. Then, while he was washing his face and brushing his hair, he asked Greg to read the book of Jonah to him out loud.

It was only four chapters long, and Greg was honored. He felt like he'd made it to a new level. Greg Laurie: Lonnie Frisbee's wingman!

He sat on the closed toilet seat lid while Lonnie brushed his hair at the bathroom sink. Greg read through the Old Testament account of the reluctant prophet who ran away from God, got swallowed and regurgitated by a large sea creature, and then preached a message of judgment and repentance to a cruel, idolatrous city named Nineveh.

While he was reading, Greg would pause occasionally and look up. Lonnie kept brushing his hair. Now and then he'd flip his head over and brush the hair down toward the floor, then flip his head back so his mane would cascade over his shoulders. He seemed to be listening, but he never took his eyes off the mirror.

Greg got to the end of Jonah. Lonnie did a few last strokes and put the brush down.

"Thanks, man!" he said.

That evening at church, Lonnie preached about Jonah to a packed house full of young people. He was electric. He gave an invitation at the end, and kids came forward, as usual.

But as Lonnie had told the story of Jonah to the crowd, Greg couldn't help but notice that his hero had gotten some of the facts messed up. He told it a bit differently than how it was laid out in the Bible.

Greg just filed it away in his head. But it didn't seem quite right. And when he went back and studied the story of Jonah and the Ninevites in the Bible, using his new commentaries, he couldn't help but notice a few things that Lonnie had left out in his funny story about Jonah getting swallowed by a whale, or a giant fish, or whatever it was.

Yes, Jonah had finally, reluctantly obeyed God. And the violent people of Nineveh, their attention galvanized by Jonah's post-whale appearance—blanched by digestive juices, he was quite a sight—had repented. God had spared their city.

And so it was for more than a century. Archeologists have found evidence of the Ninevites worshiping one God, rather than many, for a period of time. But then their polytheism, cruelty, and arrogance gradually returned. They slipped away from God, and new generations grew up. A new prophet named Nahum warned them of God's judgment, but to no avail.

In 612 BC, mighty Nineveh was assaulted by the Medes and utterly destroyed. Today it is the ancient rubble under the newer rubble of modern-day Mosul, Iraq.

Though Greg didn't really think about all that in great detail back then, he did absorb a lifelong warning from the whole biblical account of the ancient Ninevites. Repent . . . and repent as an ongoing lifestyle, so you don't fall back into your old ways.

One of the ways Greg did want to be like Lonnie Frisbee and the others in his new family was to be able to share his faith. Street evangelism was a core habit of the Jesus People at Calvary Chapel. At the time, many of the streets in interesting parts of Orange County were open season for all kinds of things. Around Newport Pier, you'd see everyone from a homeless guy playing an old guitar, its battered case open for donations, to sunburned tourists and young teens taking in the scene, to orange-robed Hare Krishnas handing out literature, to Christians talking with anyone who would listen.

Greg wanted to tell other people about Jesus, but taking a risk in a social setting was a new dynamic for him. He was used to being the mocker, not the person who might be mocked. But he'd been reading his Bible. He knew that Jesus was more important to him than what anybody else might think. And he knew that he himself had come to Christ because Lonnie cared enough to come to his high school to talk about Jesus.

The first time Greg went out to share his faith with strangers, he relied heavily on a tool that was new back then. It was a little booklet called *The Four Spiritual Laws*. It was written by Campus Crusade for Christ (now Cru) founder Bill Bright in the 1950s, and by 1970 approximately one zillion copies had been mass-produced as a bright yellow-and-black tract. It likened the physical laws of the universe to fixed spiritual truths, and boiled down the gospel message in a concise way that was easily understandable for random people on the street.

One Saturday afternoon, Greg went to Newport Beach. As his feet hit the sand, he found himself almost praying that no one would be out on the beach that day. Not good. He opened his eyes. The beach was full. The first person he saw was a middle-aged woman about the age of his mother. She had shoulder-length blonde hair parted on the side, and was sitting alone on a flowered towel.

Greg approached the towel. "Excuse me," he said. His voice seemed to be operating in a different octave than usual. "May I talk with you about God?"

"Uh, sure!" the woman said, to Greg's shock. "I'm just sitting here."

Greg sank to his knees on the sand next to her towel. He didn't know what to say, so he just pulled his bright yellow copy of *The Four Spiritual Laws* out of his pocket. He started to read the tract, word by word by word. "Just as there are physical laws that govern the physical universe, so are there spiritual laws that govern your relationship with God," he announced to the woman.

She nodded. Maybe she was humoring him.

"God loves you and offers a wonderful plan for your life," he continued. Down deep, Greg was thinking that there was absolutely no way that his robotic reading of this tract could touch this woman's heart, but when it was all over, at least he could say that he had actually "witnessed" to someone.

The lady kept listening. Greg kept reading. At the end, the booklet posed a question, something like "Is there any good reason you should not accept Jesus Christ right now?"

Reading along, Greg belatedly realized that this was a question. So he repeated it and paused for one second.

"No," said the woman.

"No what?" Greg asked.

"No, there's no reason I shouldn't accept Jesus Christ right now."

Greg's mind slowly worked through the double negative.

"What? I mean, great! Let's pray!" Greg sputtered.

He flipped through the pages of the booklet, madly looking for a prayer he could read. He found it. The lady prayed with him. There was a moment of silence. Greg didn't want to look up . . . but then the woman said, "Something just happened to me. God did something inside of me!"

Greg eventually did get more comfortable sharing his faith, as his track record as a crusade evangelist makes pretty clear. But he realized, from his very first nervous sharing of the gospel, it is not the skill or eloquence of the evangelist but the power of the Holy Spirit that opens people's hearts to recognize the truth of the gospel and yield their lives to Jesus.

As he got acclimated in this strange new world, Greg sometimes got starstruck. He was only seventeen, after all. He admired Lonnie, but Lonnie was close to his own age and easier to relate to than the older leaders like Chuck Smith. One evening Greg was at a social gathering at church, and Pastor Chuck was pouring punch. Chuck offered Greg a Dixie cup.

"Want something to drink?" Chuck asked.

"Sure," said Greg. He held out the cup. He thought it was so cool that the church leader was humbly pouring punch for his people. Then Chuck kept pouring. And pouring. Greg's cup overflowed, and then punch was streaming down his hippie sleeve, puddling on his sandals, and Chuck was laughing uncontrollably.

Even as he enjoyed the friendships in his new Christian community—Christians called it "fellowship," Greg had learned—there was one aspect of his former life that he missed. The music.

After all, his ears were used to the golden age of rock and roll. He'd loved the Beatles, the Kinks, the Rolling Stones, the Yardbirds, the Who, and the Animals. He loved Motown: Smokey Robinson, the Temptations, Diana Ross and the

Supremes, Stevie Wonder, and Marvin Gaye. And of course the Four Seasons, the Beach Boys, Buffalo Springfield, and Bob Dylan. He'd hallucinated his way through Led Zeppelin, Jimi Hendrix, Jefferson Airplane, and the Doors.

Greg, who has never lacked confidence about his own aesthetic discrimination, knew what he liked. Back then, as now, he was sure that what he preferred was in fact the gold standard of good taste. As a new convert, he was sure that every Christian song he was hearing redundantly relied on the chords G, C, D, and E minor. He sadly reflected that his days of good music were over. Well, it was a sacrifice he was willing, if not happy, to make for Jesus.

One day he was sitting in a Christian coffeehouse in Newport Beach. There was a stack of albums piled near the window with a record player next to them. He looked through the vinyl pile. No Beatles or Hendrix; instead, the album covers featured people wearing outfits that made them look like they were trying a little too hard to be cool. Folk music.

Oh well, Greg thought. Then he turned over a record cover of a guy with long, blond hair. It was called *Upon This Rock*. The guy's name was Larry Norman. He looked halfway okay.

Greg put the record on the turntable. It was good, he thought. Really good. Larry Norman had been a member of a one-hit-wonder mainstream band called People. He'd come to Christ and was now writing smart songs that were sometimes sassy, sometimes penetrating.

For Greg, it was a relief. He felt like he had at least one good Christian record to listen to.

At the time, "Christian music" was going through its own revolution, and Calvary Chapel was the epicenter of many of those changes.

There were three distinct types of music in the Calvary Chapel community. First, on Sunday mornings the congregation sang hymns that were brand-new . . . in the nineteenth century. Chuck Smith would carefully choose old hymns that amplified his Scripture message for the day, and the congregation would sing all the verses to the accompaniment of traditional organ and piano. Hippies and street kids gamely jumped right in and learned to sing along. Chuck would be attired in a traditional suit, and even Lonnie would be wearing a coat and tie.

Sunday evenings at Calvary were a different story. Lonnie would be in a flowing Jesus outfit, and Chuck would sit on a stool in comfortable clothes. He'd lead the diverse congregation a cappella in Gospel choruses sung from memory. Some were camp songs like "This Little Light of Mine," and they were soon augmented by folk songs the new Jesus People were writing, like "Alleluia," "Seek Ye First," and "Father, I Adore You." These songs of adoration, thanksgiving, and praise tended to be simple, pure, and organic. As Dr. Chuck Fromm, head of Maranatha! Music for many years, described this type of music,

> It was fashioned for an audience of one—God—or fashioned to win a lost heart. It also sometimes had a childlike hootenanny quality to it. It knew nothing of recording studios, or radio. It was musical communication, heart to heart, abandoned, lacking in self-consciousness, and imbued with passionate excitement.[1]

As formerly pagan musicians came to know Christ and wrote new stuff, there was an eventual third strand of the musical experience at Calvary Chapel. Groups would be invited to sing in prisons or at youth gatherings or in faraway churches. Their ministry on the road was going great guns, and they needed money for expenses. Ever the entrepreneur, Chuck Smith figured out a way for them to record albums and sell them so they'd have the money to travel and do ministry. From those humble beginnings, today's contemporary Christian music industry was born, a topic that deserves a book of its own.

The best known of these early groups was Love Song. This started with a group of guys who'd been playing music, together and separately, since the mid-1960s. Chuck Girard, Jay Truax, and Fred Field had played a lot of clubs, enjoyed some mainstream success, and had gotten disillusioned by the materialistic world. They'd embarked on a new spiritual quest. They'd read in Revelation about the New Jerusalem, and someone had the idea that Hawaii was absolutely where this was going to happen. They lived in caves there, ate fruit, and ingested a lot of mushrooms, but eventually got tired of waiting for the New Millennium. They came back to the mainland and formed a new band called Love Song. They played in clubs, preaching peace, love, and LSD as a path to God.

Still on their search for truth, Chuck Girard and his buddies would regularly pick up hitchhikers. Everybody did back then. The usual pattern had been that the guys they'd pick up might share some weed or LSD as an expression of thanks. Now, increasingly, the hitchhikers were sharing something else. They'd tell Chuck about how Jesus was better than any drug, and there was a hippie preacher they should go hear at a church called Calvary Chapel.

That sounded good. Chuck Girard and friends showed up one night.

Expecting Lonnie Frisbee, they heard the preaching of Chuck Smith instead. Chuck Girard realized that his spiritual search had come to an end; he gave his life to Jesus. Jay and Fred also decided to make Calvary Chapel their church home.

Chuck Smith welcomed them in.

During that time, many of the musical expressions at Calvary Chapel were earnest if not always professional. As a seasoned musician, Chuck Girard sometimes winced when he heard people up front shyly share that God had just given them a song. When they played it, he had two reactions. The first was that God had probably given them the song because He didn't want it. The second reaction was that even though the music might be substandard to his professional ear, it was still deeply moving. He sensed the presence of the Holy Spirit, and Chuck Girard was further drawn into the new community at Calvary Chapel.

A few weeks later, Chuck Smith was due to speak at an anti-drug rally. He asked his new friends, Love Song, to come and play at the event. They needed a guitar player, so they called an old friend, Tommy Coomes, who had also been checking out Christianity.

While performing with them, during the last song of the evening, "Think About What Jesus Said," Tommy found himself, in fact, thinking about what Jesus said. He realized that he hadn't made a full commitment of his life to Christ. During the song he broke down in tears, ripped off his guitar, and decided to follow Jesus. On the spot, he also decided to quit his job and move back to Orange County so he could play full time for Jesus.

Jay, Fred, Chuck, and Tommy started playing together in the spring of 1970. Love Song would morph over the years, but they made an enormous contribution to Christian music and ministry as a whole, and to Calvary Chapel in particular. They were already accomplished, professional musicians channeling influences from the Beatles, the Beach Boys, and others . . . but now their music was also a passionate vehicle for communicating their own experience of God's love and reality. Calvary Chapel, already swelling with young people, exploded with kids who heard echoes of their own search in Love Song's powerful music.

Greg felt like the Holy Spirit was present when Love Song sang; their songs took him to another place. A holy place. It was a different destination than that of his former musical heroes like Jimi Hendrix, Janis Joplin, and Jim Morrison.

During this period, people were coming to faith in great numbers at Calvary Chapel. Though reports vary, the church was baptizing about nine hundred new believers every month. Chuck Smith, Lonnie Frisbee, and other leaders would wade into the water, and crowds of people would line up to confess their sins, their new faith in Jesus, and their trust in Him. Then they'd get dunked in the cold waters of the Pacific Ocean as an outward sign of the internal reality of their new life in Christ.

One Sunday in 1971, for a reason he can no longer recall, Greg went to a different church in Orange County. He was used to church by now and felt comfortable enough to attend someplace where he didn't know anyone.

That morning Greg was wearing jeans and a loose muslin shirt with embroidery on it. His hair was long and flowing, and he had a full beard.

He got to the service a little late and realized that everyone was looking at him. He slid into a pew and looked around. Everyone there looked like they were from a television milk commercial or the set of *Ozzie and Harriet*. No long hair on men, and not a bead, bell, feather, or flower in sight.

The pastor was preaching away, but then he started addressing every sentence right at Greg, particularly as he wound down to an old-fashioned, Billy Graham–style invitation, calling anyone who wanted to come to Jesus to come forward.

The robed choir began the first verse of "Just as I Am." They were all singing to Greg. The pastor was praying, but now and then he'd peek up and look at Greg. The choir kept going. It suddenly dawned on Greg, *Oh, these people all think that they've got a real, live pagan hippie in their midst, and they so want me to come forward!* He clutched his big leather Bible, wanting to hold it up above pew level so they'd all know he was a brother.

Somewhere after about the fiftieth verse of "Just as I Am," seeing that Greg was still in his pew, the choir reluctantly drew to a halt. The pastor left the pulpit and headed straight down the aisle toward Greg.

"Son, do you know Jesus?" he asked.

"Yes," said Greg.

"Have you been baptized?"

"Yes," Greg said again.

He had passed the test.

"All right, then," the pastor said. "Do you want to come to the church picnic this afternoon?"

Greg didn't happen to attend that particular picnic, but one night he spontaneously did something that he hadn't planned, and it changed his life course. He went to a group baptism at Pirate's Cove but got there late. There were still dozens of people hanging around, though, and so he sat down with a group of kids who were playing guitars and singing.

Then he felt an irresistible urge to do something he'd never done. He'd been reading his Bible that morning, soaking up the story of a blind man whom Jesus had healed. The man's excited words from two thousand years ago were fresh, real, and echoing in Greg's head. *I once was blind, but now I see!* He felt like he just had to tell the other people about it.

This was not Greg's personality. He didn't like to take risks that had unknown social outcomes.

But he realized he had to say something.

Today Greg doesn't even remember exactly what he talked about, but the real shocker came when he finished talking. Two teenagers had joined the group, and they got his attention.

"Pastor," one of them said, "we missed the baptism earlier. We accepted Christ earlier this week. Can you baptize us?"

Greg looked around to see who they were calling pastor. He asked them to repeat what they'd said. He had no idea if he had any right to baptize people, but these kids were insistent, and he felt like Jesus was in favor of baptism. So maybe he should do it.

They waded out into the water. Greg asked the kids to declare their faith in Jesus for the forgiveness of their sins, and repeated the ritual that he had seen Pastor Chuck do many times. He managed to dunk both teenagers without drowning them.

They all waded back to the shore.

Then Greg looked up. Now there were about forty people scattered on the rocks above the cove. They were waiting for what would happen next.

All Greg could think of was a memory from his druggie days, when he'd come to Pirate's Cove and there would be this weird guy, dressed in long sleeves and long pants, preaching about Jesus. Greg had watched as people would laugh at the guy, or yell at him, or ignore him.

Now, evidently, he was that guy.

He called up to the kids sitting on the rocks, who looked like New Testament characters sitting by the Sea of Galilee. "Hey! You might be wondering why we're down here baptizing people. You might be wondering what baptism even is! The reason is, Jesus Christ, the Son of God, died on a cross and paid for our sins. He rose from the dead! And He's changed our lives!"

Greg went on. "If any of you want to, you can accept Christ as your Savior right now! Just come on down here, and I'll tell you more, and I'll pray with you."

Five or six people actually climbed down the rocks and came to the water's edge. Greg explained more about the gospel, answered their questions, and prayed with them. To his surprise, three of them decided they also wanted to be baptized right then.

Greg hadn't even turned twenty yet. But to his shock, God did something that night that set a calling on the rest of his life. He knew he wanted to be an evangelist.

14

Life as Usual, inside the Revolution

It is simply no good trying to keep any thrill. . . . Let the thrill go . . . and you will find you are living in a world of new thrills all the time. But if you decide to make thrills your regular diet and try to prolong them artificially, they will all get weaker and weaker . . . and you will be a bored, disillusioned old man for the rest of your life. It is because so few people understand this that you find many middle-aged men and women maundering about their lost youth, at the very age when new horizons ought to be appearing and new doors open all around them.

C. S. Lewis

Today when you try to describe the Jesus Movement to a young person, he or she often visualizes it as an otherworldly experience, perhaps something like flying in a plane through a hurricane, or surfing an impossibly huge blue wave, or time-traveling to the days of the early church in the book of Acts.

It did feel like each of those things, and far more. Like all movements of the Holy Spirit, the Jesus Revolution was powerful, transformational, exciting, and emotional.

For some, the experience only lasted as long as a wave. It upended them, but gradually things returned to life as usual. Some slipped back into drugs and alcohol. Some decided that they'd been mistaken about Jesus, and perhaps a different faith, or no faith at all, was what they actually preferred. All these years later, some of them write blogs that sound suspiciously bitter for someone who is so over his or her encounter with Jesus.

Some people slipped into cults. As Jesus said in the New Testament, tares grow alongside the wheat. The imitation next to the genuine. Outwardly they might have resembled the Jesus Movement people, but in reality they had nothing to do with Jesus at all. Some cults ended up as autocratic communes that cruelly abused women and children. Others removed themselves to the hills, waiting for their version of Jesus to come. Others got stuck in a time warp, repeatedly trying to relive their high-water experiences of 1970.

So, for some, the Jesus Movement was a passing wave, or a fire that soon went out. It was a non-sustainable cultural anomaly. But for uncountable numbers of baby boomers, the Jesus Revolution was a pivot point, and everything was different afterward.

Many became pastors, lay leaders, missionaries, parachurch volunteers, and powerful influences for Jesus in their communities. Many went on to birth all kinds of strong, steady ministries to help people in need and bring glory to Jesus Christ. The sustainable legacy of the Jesus Revolution—something we can all learn from—is the lives of those for whom it wasn't just a golden '70s experience that passed, but an ongoing reality rooted in the Word of God and in a healthy local church.

That's how it was for Greg. The center of the Jesus Revolution for him, circa 1970, was not starlight, rainbows, or a mystical spiritual circus. It was a decision: "Am I for Jesus or against Him?"

Then, having decided that he was *for* Jesus, the new life wasn't static. It was a journey about learning how to grow up in Christ, about an ongoing revolution of being transformed by the renewal of his mind. It was about partnering with the Holy Spirit. It was all about grace. At the same time, it involved work. Daily life was now built on practices that were as ancient as they were revolutionary: worship, the study of the Bible, prayer, fellowship, and evangelism.

When he was a teenager, Greg saw some who'd come to faith in Jesus, their faces wet with tears. Yet a few weeks later, they'd dropped away. One girl said that she just couldn't get that feeling back anymore. A guy said that his dog had gotten hit by a car, and if God had allowed that to happen, then he couldn't follow Him. Another guy confessed that he missed weed and sex too much to try to walk the straight and narrow with Jesus.

Jesus had talked about how this would happen. If the Word of God was like seed, He said, then some who hear it are like rocky ground, where the seed just can't take root. Others are like thorny ground, where the seed gets choked out by life's worries, riches, and pleasures. And others are like good soil, where the seed takes root, grows, and produces a great harvest.[1]

C. S. Lewis observed that new believers can become discouraged, right at the doorstep of faith, if they seek only the initial emotional experience, not the ongoing reality of a maturing relationship with God. Speaking in the fictional voice of a devilish tempter in *The Screwtape Letters*, he wrote,

> The Enemy [God] allows this disappointment to occur on the threshold of every human endeavor. . . . The Enemy takes this risk because He has a curious fantasy of making all these disgusting little human vermin into what He calls His "free" lovers and servants—"sons" is the word He uses. . . . Desiring their freedom, He therefore refuses to carry them, by their mere affections and habits, to any of the goals which He sets before them: He leaves them to "do it on their own." And there lies our opportunity. But also, remember, there lies our danger. If once they get through this initial dryness successfully, they become much less dependent on emotion and therefore much harder to tempt.[2]

Perhaps his early days of faith were easier for Greg in this respect because he wasn't expecting a big rush of ongoing emotion to carry him onward in his new life. During his formative years, he'd been disappointed time and time again, and had learned that he probably wouldn't experience a whole lot of warm and fuzzy feelings. He was a pretty fact-oriented person. And in his new life, he wanted to reach out to people like he had been. Cynical. Suspicious. Mad at the world. From broken homes. People who had dreamed the hippie dream of peace, love, and understanding, or some other mythology, and hadn't found any of those things.

He was a spiritual sponge, poring over the pages of his new Bible and questioning people who had been reading it longer than he had. He also had access to a new, cutting-edge technology to help him with his learning curve: cassette tapes.

He listened to hours and hours of sermons and Bible studies. He bought the books that Chuck Smith recommended, mostly the classic commentaries by Martyn Lloyd-Jones, C. H. Spurgeon, H. A. Ironside, W. H. Griffith Thomas, G. Campbell Morgan, and many more.

Aside from wondering why so many commentators used their initials rather than their full names, Greg loved studying their work. He was finding that his creative powers, formerly dulled by his dope use, were coming back in full force. He could concentrate. He'd never had any interest in school, but this was different. Studying the Bible was focusing himself on something that was alive and actually had the power to change him.

In addition, Greg was learning some other habits. Though his mother had been a hard worker in her day job, her use of alcohol had blunted her ability to instill a strong work ethic and other vigorous habits in her son. Greg felt like he'd been raised by wolves, with no cues or clues about healthy living. In Chuck Smith—and others—Greg saw the adult figure he'd unconsciously been looking for.

Out of the pulpit, Chuck wasn't a big talker. He taught by doing. Greg learned the value of working hard, being on time, finishing projects, and taking the initiative. One day Chuck had just conducted a wedding, and then, during the reception, a pipe burst. Dirty water flooded the festivities. People were running around, wringing their hands. Chuck took off his suit jacket, folded it on a chair, and went to get some tools. Then he knelt in the flooded area, dealt with the faulty pipe, and fixed the leak.

Another man who had a huge effect on fatherless Greg was an unlikely character named Laverne Romaine. He was a former Marine drill sergeant with large glasses and a body shaped a little bit like a fire hydrant. He loved the church and loved the hippies, though their culture was the opposite of his crew-cut military background. "The world as I knew it has been encompassed by more hair than you can shake a stick at," he'd say with a grin.

He saw himself as an Aaron to Chuck Smith's Moses, meaning that his role was to support what Chuck was doing at Calvary Chapel. In his dry, no-nonsense way, he'd say things like:

> An assistant pastor is there to support the senior pastor, full-on, full-out, without grumbling. . . . Whether the need is to clean toilets or to teach Bible studies, they are there to help. Who is an assistant supposed to help? Anyone. An assistant is not "on the clock." He is not a member of a "pastor's union." As an assistant, you are not the senior pastor's buddy. You are to leave after taking care of all the basic needs of the church and everything is done that needs to be done. This often will mean leaving the church grounds long after the senior pastor has gone home. You are to be a Timothy, someone who does not seek his own interests, but those of Jesus Christ.[3]

Understandably, no one called this guy Laverne. He was "Romaine," a gruff but kindly presence, checking up on anyone and everyone to see how they were doing, if they were following Jesus or slipping back into old ways, or if they needed a hand. He coddled no one; he supported everyone.

In similar ways, Kay Smith modeled basic virtues for girls who had run away from home or had lacked training about living in a pure and purposeful way. For kids who'd been short on role models, the combination of sound Bible teaching, a loving community of believers, and the challenge to grow in new ways was irresistible.

As Greg finished his senior year of high school, he didn't have the money or a strong desire to go to college. His main interest was to simply learn more and more of the Scriptures. He could do that by studying his heart out on his own, and spending more and more time learning from the pastors at Calvary Chapel.

After his graduation, Greg was eligible for the draft, and the Vietnam War was still sucking young men into the jungles of Southeast Asia. As a nonbeliever, he hadn't been a draft card–burning ideologue. He was just a kid who didn't understand what this seemingly endless war was even about, or why some of his friends had come home in coffins. He had no interest in participating.

But by the time he became eligible for the draft, he'd had a huge change of perspective about everything. He now knew he held dual citizenship. By birth, he was a citizen of the United States of America. By his new birth, his higher allegiance now was as a citizen of the kingdom of God. No longer a glib rebel, he'd sought counsel with Calvary pastors, prayed, and studied Romans 13 and other biblical passages. He spoke with Pastor Romaine, the former Marine; Romaine counseled him that the Bible directed Greg to submit to his civil government unless it was directly opposing or suppressing the gospel. So, instead of protesting or trying to get out of the draft, he figured that if God allowed him to be called up, then God must have a purpose to somehow use him in Vietnam.

This was a seismic shift in thinking for Greg. During his chaotic childhood, he'd had to protect himself, because no one else was going to look out for him. Self-preservation was the overarching goal. Now he belonged to Christ. God had a claim on his life and a plan for it. Figuring out what he, Greg, wanted was simply not the first priority anymore.

It was strange and liberating.

Greg ended up with a very high draft number. He wasn't called up for military service.

Meanwhile, Greg had gotten a reputation around Calvary as a skilled cartoonist because of a tract he'd designed after he heard Chuck Smith preach about Jesus and a woman He met at a well. "Everyone who drinks this water will be thirsty again," Jesus said, "but whoever drinks the water I give them will never thirst. Indeed, the water I give them will become in them a spring of water welling up to eternal life."[4]

The tract was called "Living Water." Chuck Smith loved it so much he had five thousand copies printed. Those were gone in a week. Within a year, three hundred thousand copies had been printed. "Living Water" became a huge evangelism tool for the Calvary Chapel community.

Around this time, Greg met a guy named Kerne Erickson. Kerne was an artist too, but not self-taught like Greg. He'd been trained at the prestigious Art Center College of Design in Pasadena where the Disney people recruited much of their talent. Kerne told Greg that he was living with a couple of other Christian artists in a house in Santa Ana. They began each day with prayer and Bible study, and they all encouraged each other to produce art for the glory of God. Kerne invited Greg to move in with them.

That sounded like Christian nirvana to Greg.

He went home that night; his mom was there, but she'd been drinking, as usual. So he went to bed. The next day he told her that the time had come for him to move out, as they had different friends, interests, and goals.

To Greg's surprise, tears welled up in his mother's eyes. He hadn't thought she would care if he came or went; after all, she never hugged him or seemed particularly glad to see him. He felt like a potted plant in her home.

He realized Charlene's tears were a product of shock rather than sadness or love for Greg. Up until this point, *she'd* been the one who left. She'd left husband after husband, relationship after relationship. Maybe she couldn't quite believe that the one man who had been with her for most of the past eighteen tumultuous years was moving on.

Greg gathered his few belongings. Back at the house with Kerne and the guys, his bedroom was a converted garage with a cot. He loved it, and he loved the life of being a "starving artist," except for the starving part. No one had any money, and dinner was usually an exotic mixture of elbow macaroni, pickles, ketchup, and old ground beef when they could afford it.

Greg somehow acquired an exotic parrot during this time period and arranged an elaborate macramé perch hanging above his bed. It looked very artistic when the bright bird would pose on its perch. The only problem was that Greg ended up sleeping in feathers and occasional bird poop.

When he wasn't plucking feathers off his jeans or designing Bible tracts or posters, Greg spent his time at Calvary Chapel. He'd do whatever odd jobs needed to be done and scope around for food. He'd study the Bible, talk with new Christians, evangelize on the street, answer the phones, run errands, and pray with people who were going through hard times. Watching Chuck Smith and the other pastors, he learned how to be available to the Holy Spirit and available to other people.

During that time period, one of Greg's most cherished possessions was a surprise letter he'd gotten, care of Calvary Chapel.

It was scrawled in pencil on plain paper, and was accompanied by a grimy copy of the "Living Water" tract.

A while ago I was given a little booklet entitled "Living Water." I read it and thought it was good but put it away with some letters and forgot about it. One day I found it again and started to read it. As I read I felt God was talking to me and I began to understand that I needed Him and I should follow Him. Now I am sending this booklet back to you with the hope that you will give it to someone who hasn't quite found his way back to Christ yet.[5]

Greg would have loved the letter just for what it was. But when he looked at the envelope, the return address made it even more meaningful.

San Quentin State Prison.

Greg treasured that letter for a long time. It was a tangible reminder for him . . . not only of the spiritual prison God had freed him from, but the fact that God was using him, an eighteen-year-old knucklehead, to pass that spiritual freedom on to others.

15

No Bare Feet Allowed!

The gospel is meant to comfort the afflicted and afflict the comfortable.

A well-known adaptation of a 1902 quote by journalist
Finley Peter Dunne

As Calvary Chapel continued to grow, the congregation bought a property in Santa Ana and built a grand new building on it. They had been thinking big: it could hold three hundred people. It was also decorated in the latest design trends the early 1970s had to offer: avocado-green shag carpeting and burnt-orange cushions on the pews. There were even new wooden cup holders on the back of each pew to accommodate everyone's little plastic communion cups.

On the first Sunday in their brand-new building, the church was packed. Kids were sitting in every available scrap of floor space. Chuck Smith assumed that things would level off as the novelty of the new facility wore off.

But the next Sunday, there were even more people. More and more hippies were coming to faith, and they were pouring into Calvary Chapel. There were a lot of other new people too—judges, police officers, parents, school administrators, and others who'd been drawn in by the news that formerly troubled young people were being transformed by God, and it was happening in this church. Many of the visitors ended up staying themselves.

It was wonderful.

Still, there were problems in paradise.

The church deacons were worried: there were so many barefoot hippies attending church, and the oil from their feet was going to damage and soil the new carpeting. And shag, while popular for many reasons that are still unknown, was notoriously impossible to deep clean. To add insult to injury, the barefoot kids were hooking their toes into the communion cup racks on non-communion mornings.

The following Sunday, Pastor Chuck got to church a little earlier than usual. He was surprised to see a large sign in front of the church entrance.

"NO BARE FEET ALLOWED!" It was signed by the church board members.

Chuck nearly passed out on the front steps of his own church. He ripped down the sign. He rushed inside and eventually found the sign committee.

"Do you mean to say," he burst out to them, "because we have this beautiful new carpet, we've got to say to kids that they can't come into our church because they have bare feet?

"Let's rip up the carpet, then!" Chuck went on. "Let's just have concrete floors! Are we going to say to kids that they can't come in here because they have dirty clothes, and they might mess up our nice, new upholstered pews? Then let's just get wooden benches! Let's never, ever, turn a person away from church!

"Think about it!" Chuck concluded. "We—the older, established Christians—are on trial. We quote Scriptures like 1 John 4:7 [about loving one another] and James 2 [about not showing favoritism for those dressed well over those who are shabby], but the actions we took today stamp a question mark across our faith. In times like this, we need to search ourselves for the motivations that are controlling and guiding our actions!"[1]

There were no more signs banning bare feet or anything else. The church doubled in size. The leadership decided to hold two, and then three, separate services. People sat on the patio outside.

So Chuck and his team found a huge circus tent, which was probably appropriate, and pitched it on their corner of Greenville Street and Sunflower Avenue in Santa Ana. Late on Saturday evening, before their first tent Sunday, workers were putting up the lights and lining up sixteen hundred folding chairs. Chuck said to one of his colleagues, "Well, how long do you suppose it will take the Lord to fill this tent?"

His friend laughed and looked at his watch. "We'll know in about ten more hours, brother!"

And ten hours later, on Sunday morning, they stood and watched the people stream in. The first of their services was at 8:00 a.m. Standing room only. The same thing happened at the next service. All kinds of people, whether newly converted hippies or folks who'd been in church all their lives, were excited about what God was doing through His Word at Calvary Chapel.

They would meet there for two years while they built an even bigger permanent building to hold their multiplying flock. During that period, the architect had to enlarge the plans three separate times so the completed new building could accommodate its church. The people.

On Sunday mornings, the church was full of conservative adults wearing their Sunday best like they had for decades. Still, kids with long hair, shorts, and sandals flooded the place. They'd sit for an hour with their Bibles opened as Pastor Chuck, Kenn Gulliksen, Don McClure, Tom Stipe, or one of the other pastors would teach a detailed study of a section of Scripture.

On Sunday evenings, Pastor Chuck wore more casual clothes—though he didn't try to be a hipster—and the music was fresh. So fresh, in fact, that a lot of it had just been written, like Love Song's "Little Country Church," which was hot off the griddle when the band played it one Sunday evening, singing about how people weren't "as stuffy as they were before." Instead, they just wanted to praise the Lord, work for revival, and come together, people with "long hair, short hair, some coats and ties . . . lookin' past the hair and straight into the eyes."[2]

The lyrics captured Calvary Chapel at the time. It was a body of believers made up of old people and young people, new Christians and people who'd been following Jesus for a while. It surely was not perfect, but the people loved and accepted each other. They loved Jesus, were eternally grateful to Him, and wanted to consume His Word. In mainstream culture in those chaotic days, people might be divided by labels: hippie or straight, cool kid or loser, rich or poor, black or white. But in the church, those divisions fell away.

16

"Yes, *That* Jesus!"

I rejoice in the decided conviction that this is the Lord's doing; unaccountable by any natural causes, entirely above and beyond what any human device or power could produce; an outpouring of the Spirit of God upon God's people, quickening them to greater earnestness in his service; and upon the unconverted, to make them new creatures in Christ Jesus.

Bishop Charles P. McIlvaine (1799–1873)

By 1971, Cathe Martin had reached the ripe age of fourteen and made the transition from cute Catholic schoolgirl to a happy, hazy hippie. Her family had made the move from Kuala Lumpur to Long Beach, and to her parents' dismay, they discovered that the drug culture was at least as bad in Southern California as it had been in Malaysia. Cathe's older sisters quickly figured out where the drug action and the cool guys were, and by now Cathe was ready to join them.

She loved the gentle edges and mellow colors of smoking dope. She and her sisters would hitchhike to love-ins at local parks, where they'd sit on the grass, smoke some weed, and talk with whoever came by about music or life or flowers. She loved wearing long granny dresses and going barefoot. But she could not escape the guilt that plagued her, along with a deep desire in her heart for something more.

One spring day the Martin girls went to a concert at Long Beach College. They didn't know anything about the bands that would be performing, but it sounded like a cool scene. Cathe was in ninth grade. They were sitting outside in a park, smoking pot under some palm trees, when some long-haired guys came over to say hello. It wasn't unusual; one thing Cathe loved about hippie culture was that everyone shared everything. There weren't any lines dividing people like she'd experienced growing up.

"Hey," Cathe's sister said. "You guys want to sit down and get high with us?"

"Thanks," one of them responded. "We used to do all that. But we're not into dope anymore."

That seemed weird to Cathe. "Why not?" she asked.

"Well," the guy said, "we found out what we were really looking for. We'd been looking for some kind of higher consciousness, you know, and we thought drugs were the way to get there. But we found out how to really find God, and now we have a relationship with Jesus."

Cathe had never heard of anything like that. She'd gone to church as a child, and she'd never seen anyone there who seemed like he or she was a friend of God. Church seemed like it was just about going through a bunch of rituals that didn't get you to the mystical connection with God that Cathe longed for. So what did this guy mean about a "relationship with Jesus"?

"You mean Jesus Christ?" she asked. "Are you serious?"

"Yes, *that* Jesus." The guy laughed. "We found out that Jesus isn't mad; He loves everybody, and He paid the penalty for the bad stuff that every single person does. The penalty was death. So He died in my place, in your place. But He didn't stay dead, because He was God. He came back to life. And everyone who believes in Him and asks for forgiveness of their sins and trusts in Him will live forever!"

Cathe had never heard something that wild. Her face got red and her mouth was open, and then suddenly she thought that this guy was just kidding with her, trying to get her going. *I'm the youngest person in this circle*, she thought, *and he's just trying to trick me.* She pulled back and started laughing, her hands over her face.

"Wait a minute," the guy said. "What I'm telling you is true!"

Cathe didn't want to embarrass herself by seeming gullible. But even as she stood there giggling, her hands over her eyes, the thought crossed her mind: *My life is a wreck. And here I am, on my way right to hell, laughing, and what these guys are telling us is actually right and real and true.*

She stopped laughing. "Okay," she said. "If God is real, tell me what I have to do to have a relationship with Him, like you said before. Is it really that simple?"

The guys nodded. "Just come into the concert with us," they said. "You'll see how simple it is in there."

Cathe and her sisters walked with them into the auditorium. Up front on the stage was an acid rock band called Agape. They played a few songs that might have been about Jesus, but Cathe couldn't really tell, because the electric guitars were so loud she couldn't hear any lyrics.

After the first set, one of the band members stood up front and told the crowd about Jesus, and how whoever wanted to receive Him could become a son or daughter of God right there.

"Is there anyone here who wants to have a relationship with God through Jesus Christ?" he asked. "If you do, just stand up and come down to the front of the stage."

I have to stand up, Cathe thought. *That's what I want.*

She went up to the front. As far as she could tell, she was the only fourteen-year-old in the room, and now here she was with all these college students, accepting Jesus. She prayed with some people who were there to help the new believers. One of them gave her a Bible. The guys who had brought Cathe and her sisters to the concert gave Cathe a hug. "This is so great!" one of them said. "We'll take you to church with us tomorrow so you can start learning more about walking with Jesus!"

As Cathe and her sisters left the college campus, she felt like she was one of maybe ten people on the entire planet who had ever felt the way she felt. She felt clean inside. Forgiven. Special. God loved her.

When the girls got home, they told their parents that they were going to church the next morning. That was new. Pilar and Dick Martin didn't quite know what to think, but church was a lot better than anywhere else their daughters had been going lately.

The next day a dented, rusty beater car slowly pulled up in front of the Martin home. One of the Christian guys the girls had met the day before got out. He had on jeans, love beads, and a torn strip from a cotton T-shirt wrapped around his forehead as a makeshift headband for his long, curly hair.

He'd written "Agape" on it in black magic marker, and if the effect was not particularly artistic, it was sincere.

The beater car somehow made it from Long Beach all the way to Calvary Chapel in Costa Mesa. The sanctuary was overflowing with hippies, old people, and everyone in between. There were hundreds of people sitting on folding chairs outside.

Oh my gosh! Cathe thought. *I guess I'm not just one of ten people in the whole world who know Jesus!*

After an old guy called Pastor Chuck talked about the Bible, a hippie came out who looked like Jesus. Lonnie Frisbee. He asked anyone who wanted to know Jesus to come forward. Cathe stood up again and made her way to the front with a few dozen other people, thinking that this must be what you do every time you come to church.

Lonnie led everyone in a prayer, and then Pastor Chuck clearly explained what it meant to follow Jesus, and how to read the Bible and learn more about Him. *Wow*, Cathe thought. *It's not all mystical and trippy. It really makes sense. It's a cool way to live.*

After church, Cathe told her parents where they had been and what they had done. "Nooooooo!" her mother moaned. "What are you doing? You went to a *Protestant* church? It must be a cult!"

"Mom!" Cathe said. "You've been praying and getting the nuns to pray for us for so long. You've been asking God to change us. And now we're done with drugs and all that other stuff. Jesus is the only way we can really change!"

Pilar and Dick didn't know quite what to think of their daughters' new allegiances. But like parents across America, they were both thankful for—and mystified by—the Jesus Revolution.

17

Love Story

WANTED:

JESUS CHRIST, ALIAS: THE MESSIAH, THE SON OF GOD, KING OF KINGS, LORD OF LORDS, PRINCE OF PEACE, ETC.

Notorious leader of an underground liberation movement. . . .

APPEARANCE: Typical hippie type—long hair, beard, robe, sandals.

Hangs around slum areas, few rich friends, often sneaks out into the desert.

BEWARE: This man is extremely dangerous.

His insidiously inflammatory message is particularly dangerous to young people who haven't been taught to ignore him yet.

He changes men and claims to set them free.

Time, June 21, 1971

No doubt in honor of Cathe Martin's conversion, *Time* magazine published an unusual cover story a few weeks later.

The magazine's cover was a pop-art-style illustration of a radical-looking Jesus and the name of His movement that was sweeping through youth culture: "The Jesus Revolution."

In a style that is inconceivable in our own day, *Time*'s writers gushed, "Jesus is alive and well and living in the radical spiritual fervor of a growing number of young Americans who have proclaimed an extraordinary religious revolution in his name." *Time* continued,

> Their message: the Bible is true, miracles happen, God really did so love the world that he gave it his only begotten son. . . .
>
> Bibles abound, whether the cherished, fur-covered King James Version or scruffy, back-pocket paperbacks, they are invariably well-thumbed and often memorized. . . . There is an uncommon morning freshness to this movement, a buoyant atmosphere of hope and love along with the usual rebel zeal. . . . But their love seems more sincere than a slogan, deeper than the fast-fading sentiments of the flower children; what startles the outsider is the extraordinary sense of joy that they are able to communicate.[1]

Time's cover story was much broader than just what was happening in Southern California. But for the young people who were coming to faith in Costa Mesa and beyond, the writers had gotten it right.

Soon after Cathe's first trip to Calvary Chapel, she was baptized at Pirate's Cove in Corona del Mar. She learned about opportunities to grow in her new relationship with Jesus and made her way, with her sisters, to a Bible study one Monday night at a coffeehouse in Long Beach. As they walked in, the people were singing a song that Cathe had heard in church:

155

Love, love, love, love
the gospel in a word is love
love your neighbor as your brother
love, love, love love.[2]

It was so simple, but when everyone sang it in a round, with different parts, it was beautiful, haunting, and pure. Cathe held her new Bible on her lap as the teacher came up front to lead the study. She wasn't surprised that he was young; she was used to Lonnie Frisbee, and this guy was just a few years younger than Lonnie. He wore a pair of faded blue jeans and a T-shirt, and had blond hair past his shoulders and a red beard. Cathe thought he was cute.

The guy's name was Greg. He sat on a stool up front, his Bible on his lap, his leg bouncing up and down with barely suppressed energy, like there was a coiled spring inside of him. At this point Cathe still had some hippie cobwebs in her brain; she loved vague, mystical vibrations. Brother Sun, Sister Moon, feel-good moments. But this red-bearded Greg guy wasn't like that. He was direct. He made the Bible so real and applicable to Cathe. His personality was inquisitive, quick, and funny. He was so good at clearing clutter and cutting to the main points. He was a genius, she thought. Or maybe he was crazy.

After the study was over and people were milling around, this Greg guy came straight over to Cathe and her sisters. "Are you going to come back?" he asked. "Did you like the Bible study? Are you coming to Calvary Chapel? Do you want to get some coffee?"

Caffeine, Cathe thought. *That's the last thing this guy needs.*

Gradually Cathe and her sisters started hanging out with Greg after Bible study. He took pains to be equally attentive to all three of them, but it was pretty clear that he had a special interest in Cathe. Her sisters kidded her about it, but they liked him and thought this new relationship was a good thing for their little sister.

Eventually, Greg invited Cathe to drive with him to Calvary Chapel's summer camp at Idyllwild Pines, a retreat center southwest of Palm Springs. It was a rustic lodge that had been founded as a Christian retreat center back in 1923. It had woods, meadows, hiking trails, a creek, stone fireplaces, old cabins, and a pool.

The getaway wasn't a designated retreat for just one segment of the church, like the youth group or singles or seniors or families. It was for the whole Calvary Chapel community. The idea was to sing silly camp songs, swim, hike, play games, eat burned bacon and high-carb retreat food, and worship God and study His Word together. It sounded like a little piece of Heaven for Cathe.

Cathe and Greg packed their stuff into Greg's little 1960-something Corvair, which had its two-speed gearshift mounted on the dashboard, its engine in the back, and an eccentric personality. Greg had bought it for $225. It had had an unfortunate crash into the back of a Cadillac, and had gotten the worse end of the deal. So its headlights were crossed, making it look a bit like Jerry Lewis in *The Nutty Professor.*

Cathe had been thinking of him as a friend she really liked, but Greg, in his usual direct way, now wanted to use their time in the Nutty Corvair to talk about their relationship.

"So I guess we're boyfriend and girlfriend now," he announced to her as the cross-eyed vehicle sputtered along the highway. "And there's one thing we should be clear about. I just want you to know that if you ever get between me and my relationship with God, it's over. And the same is true for you. We've both got to seek God first, and then He'll show us where our relationship is supposed to go."

Cathe had never, ever had a guy say something like that to her. It was refreshing. She hated it when guys were wishy-washy and didn't really know what they thought or where they were going. She wanted someone who was comfortable in his own skin and sure of his convictions and calling. Young as she was, she also knew that she did not want to be the center of anyone's life. It was suffocating. Greg's clarity about putting Jesus first made her feel secure.

Also, Cathe was drawn to Greg because he was so different from her own father. She deeply loved her dad, but like many men of his generation he was very reserved, a controlled man who didn't readily express feelings or emotion. As an oil company executive who'd lived all over the world, he was also very dignified and polished in his manners.

Greg, on the other hand, was like a strange force of nature. He questioned everything, overflowed with energy, and was constantly bursting into fake operatic voices or silly songs. Because he was easily bored, he was never boring. Later she would discover that most successful comedians actually come from severely troubled childhoods and develop humor as a coping mechanism at an early age. That explained a lot about Greg. Cathe never knew quite what to expect, but he was an intriguing mix of deep spiritual commitment and crazy fun.

By the time Greg and Cathe arrived at the camp, it was very late. There were no lights at the entrance, and the cross-eyed Corvair didn't do much to illuminate the night. They got out of the car, dragging their sleeping bags, going from building to building, looking for somebody, anybody, to tell them where the guys' and girls' cabins were. All quiet on the camp front. Not a guitar, not a "Praise the Lord," nothing. Everyone was asleep.

They didn't want to ring the dinner bell and rouse the whole camp. So after about forty-five minutes of searching, they finally found one lodge building that was unlocked. It was empty . . . except for a few cots on one side of the big main room and a few cots on the other.

Greg got his sleeping bag and rolled it out on the farthest cot on one side.

Cathe rolled hers out on the farthest cot on the other.

They each climbed in their respective bag, fully clothed. Eventually they went to sleep. An hour or so later, Cathe woke in the dark to hear fragmented words and thrashing. It was Greg, across the room. "Noooooooooo!" he was saying. "Couldn't find anywhere else to sleep! Just waiting for someone to come and show us where we're s'posed to stay!"

After a second, Cathe got what was going on, and she eventually went back to sleep. It was just Greg's conscience speaking to whoever was in charge of the retreat, explaining that everything was on the up and up.

The next morning, Chuck Smith had asked Greg to lead a little devotional for the big group. Greg was anxious to share from the Word, but he was also nervous. He sat on a stool at the front of the rustic meeting room, his Bible open to Ephesians 6.

"Therefore, take up the whole armor of God," Greg began. He continued through the passage, which described the various spiritual weapons that the believer has available to withstand temptation and trials. "Stand . . . taking the shield of faith, with which you will be able to quench all the fiery darts of the wicked one."

The only problem with this wonderful Scripture was that when jittery Greg read that last phrase, it came out of his mouth as something about "quenching all the diary farts of the wicked one."

He didn't quite realize what had happened until there was a huge explosion of snorting glee, and Chuck Smith almost had to be scraped off the floor, he was laughing so hard.

Yep, thought Cathe, *it's never dull around Greg*. But he also absolutely drove her crazy.

They were both strong-minded, opinionated people, and they fought a lot. Cathe realized, though, that while she fought for the sake of an argument, Greg fought because he wanted to find out what was really true. Interesting. The problem was, what they were fighting about was inconsequential and usually unprovable. Which band had the best music. Which route they should take to drive to church. Which was better, crunchy or creamy peanut butter.

"Why would I ever want to be around you?" Cathe would yell at Greg when the tension got too high. "You're impossible!" Then she'd break up with him.

But down deep Cathe knew why she wanted to be around him. He was the first guy she'd ever met who really knew what he wanted to do with his life. Even when they'd fight, she knew that the bottom line was that he actually wanted to do the right thing, whatever it was. In comparison to Greg, other guys seemed so flimsy; they'd blow whichever way the group wanted to go. Greg was different. If only he would stop driving her crazy.

At one point they broke up. "That's it!" Cathe exploded. "I am done. Done."

Around that time, Greg was preparing to leave town for the summer. He waited for Cathe to cool off a little and then sent her a card. It featured the Puritan-looking guy from a Quaker Oats commercial from the 1960s, which Greg and Cathe had both seen about a million times when they were kids.

In it, against a backdrop of howling winter winds and freezing snow, the Quaker Oats man proclaims, "Nothing is better for me than thee!" He is addressing a steaming bowl of oatmeal . . . but Greg thought his sentiments might warm Cathe's heart and make her yearn for him.

Not quite. After a terse note telling him not to write her anymore, there was nothing but a frosty silence from Cathe.

So Greg sadly left for his trip, deciding he may as well get on with his life. Because the Jesus Movement had created an atmosphere where young people were quite open to hearing the gospel, Greg and his fellow hippie preachers would hit the road regularly. They'd travel with a band and hold services at churches and community centers up and down the West Coast. So on this particular extended excursion, Greg was the designated speaker, and he was with a four-person band that included a married couple and a single young woman who sang and played guitar.

On the road, it was soon assumed that Greg and the single songstress would end up as a couple. Back at home, Cathe started assuming that too. *Well,* she thought, *that's probably good. She's so godly, and she can sing, and she can talk up front. She's so cute. She'd be a great partner for him. And he and I just fight all the time!*

But the more she thought about it, the more her prayer life was enhanced. Finally it came down to this: "Oh God!" Cathe told the Lord. "I know Greg and I fight like crazy, but there's no one like him. I feel like he really is for me. But I want what you want . . . so if you want us to be together, I pray that you would bring him home, off the road, this coming weekend."

Greg wasn't scheduled to return until the end of the summer. But the next Sunday after her prayer, Cathe walked into Calvary Chapel and there he was.

Cathe was in her usual outfit: a long, flowing batik-print dress, equally flowing thick, blonde hair, and a little pair of pink granny glasses perched on her nose. She'd made a few changes since Greg had left, though. For one, she'd gone a little less au naturel regarding her eyebrows.

She saw Greg making his way toward her as she chatted with a group of friends. "What are *you* doing here?" she asked him sweetly.

Greg said nothing. He was just staring at her face. Silently.

"What?" Cathe sputtered.

Now everyone in the circle was gazing at Cathe's face. Finally, Greg was able to get a few words out.

"You plucked your eyebrows!" he pronounced.

And just like that, they were back together.

18

Billy Graham's
Good Vibrations

Let us not be satisfied with the religious mediocrity of our age. The New Testament church, the zeal of the New Testament Christians is our example. Join us in expecting God to perform a miracle in our hearts as we make ourselves available to Him and all that He has to teach us during this coming week.

Bill Bright, regarding Explo '72

In the fall of 1971, Billy Graham released a book, one of the thirty-three he wrote over the course of his long life. Graham had become America's best-known religious leader, a role he had held, and would hold, for decades. Greg had not met him yet—that would come later—but they were both focused on the same thing: the Jesus Revolution. With its pop-art-style cover and One Way salute, Graham's book about *The Jesus*

Generation struck a chord, selling two hundred thousand copies within the first two weeks of its release.

Graham wrote about the hippie culture's rejection of conventional cultural values. Some had chosen political protest; others had simply dropped out and dropped acid. Others had attempted to create countercultural communes and "get back to the garden." Others had adopted a new set of life principles—based in a vague existential relativism—that were as far from their parents' absolutes of right and wrong as they could flee.

And many others, said Billy Graham, had found the one revolution that was different: it was not about a new set of life principles, but a Person. "Tens of thousands of American youth are caught up in it. They are being 'turned on' to Jesus," Graham wrote.[1] He said that he'd been bombarded with questions about this new spiritual phenomenon in the mail, at press conferences, on Capitol Hill, at the White House, and in the editorial boardrooms of the *New York Times*, the *Chicago Tribune*, and other news outlets of the day.

Graham hoped that readers who hadn't yet joined the revolution—those who were experiencing, in his words, "bad vibrations"—would come to faith in Christ and join in as well.

Of course it had not been a perfect revolution. "There are pitfalls," Graham wrote. "There are fears. There are critics. Some say it is too superficial—and in some cases it is. Some say it is too emotional—and in some cases it is. Some say it is outside the established church—and in some cases it is."

But, said Dr. Graham, the early church in the book of Acts had such weaknesses as well. In his analysis, the new Jesus Movement also had some intriguing strengths.

- It was *spontaneous*, without a human figurehead or leader. It was centered around Jesus himself. Graham quoted *Look*, a national bi-weekly magazine with a circulation of about six million. Its reporters had written of the Jesus People, "All the Christians agree Christ is the great common denominator of the movement. He brings everyone together."

- The Jesus Revolution was *Bible based*. The majority of the Jesus People were not simply drawn to a vague appreciation of Jesus, but dug into well-worn Bibles for their understanding of Christ, His teaching, and His death and resurrection.

- The movement was about an *experience* with Jesus Christ, not head knowledge. The Jesus People emphasized that people must be born again, experiencing the transforming power of the Holy Spirit.

- Graham went on to cite the movement's emphasis on the *Holy Spirit*. Years earlier, he said, he'd asked distinguished theologian Karl Barth what the new emphasis in theology would be in the next twenty years. Dr. Barth had responded immediately, "The Holy Spirit!" "Little did I dream," Dr. Graham wrote in *The Jesus Generation*, "that [this] would come through a youth revival in America!"

- Next, young people who came to Christ in this time period were *finding a cure* from drugs, other addictions, and ingrained patterns of sin. Their lives were dramatically transformed.

- The movement's emphasis was on Christian *discipleship*. It wasn't just about wearing crosses and other

Jesus gear, or slapping One Way stickers on Volkswagen vans. The Jesus People understood, because of their focus on the Bible and the Holy Spirit, that salvation was in fact followed by a lifetime of sanctification, or becoming more like Jesus over the long run.

- It was *interracial and multiethnic.* The Jesus People had come of age in a society reeling from segregation and social partitions. They saw in their Bibles that in Jesus, there were no racial divisions. They believed it.

- The movement showed a great zeal for *evangelism.* Billy Graham noted that Jesus Christ's last words on earth were, "Go forth to every part of the world and proclaim the Good News," and in the book of Acts, that's exactly what the "original Jesus people, most of them young," went out and did in the first century. The same was true of the new, young believers about 1,970 years later.

- The movement emphasized the *second coming* of Jesus Christ. Reflecting the times that the Jesus People grew up in, Graham wrote that "these young people don't put much stock in the old slogans of the New Deal, the Fair Deal, the New Frontier, and the Great Society. They believe that utopia will arrive only when Jesus returns. Thus these young people are on sound biblical ground."

Because of Graham's huge influence on conservative Christians, his focus on the Jesus Movement served as an important wake-up call for older believers who might have otherwise ignored what was going on in youth culture. It was also a signal that what had started primarily as a hippie phenomenon was becoming more mainstream. It was giving fresh energy to the work of parachurch ministries that had been working among young people for years, like Fellowship of Christian Athletes (FCA), Campus Crusade for Christ (Cru), InterVarsity Christian Fellowship (IV), Young Life, Youth for Christ (YFC), and the Navigators, among others. Most of these were born in the burgeoning evangelical movement of the 1930s and '40s, adapted during the tumult and new expressions of the '60s and '70s, and continue to do great outreach and discipleship today.

If the Jesus Movement started as a spontaneous movement among hippies, Billy Graham helped to shape its second wave as traditionally conservative Christians got on board. The clearest manifestation of that was Explo '72, a gathering of about eighty thousand young people in Dallas in August of that year.

A "religious Woodstock," it was organized by Bill Bright's Campus Crusade for Christ and was at the time the largest religious camp meeting ever to take place in the United States. University students, high school kids, and young people from across the country arrived in buses, broken-down cars, and flower-power vans to spend five days in evangelism, discipleship training, worship, and outreach to the city of Dallas. They were mostly white, clean-cut, and middle class. They yelled Jesus cheers, raised their pointed index fingers in the era's famous One Way sign, and enjoyed bands from Johnny Cash to Love Song to Larry Norman to praise and worship music.

President Richard Nixon had indicated that he'd love an invitation to join the kids, perhaps as a photo opportunity to appear in solidarity with at least one aspect of youth culture. Concerned that his presence would politicize the event, the event planners wisely declined to accommodate the president's wishes. Though no one knew it at the time, the Watergate break-in had already occurred, the cover-up was well underway, and Nixon's presidency would soon topple altogether.

The *New York Times* called Explo '72 "the largest and most conspicuous public outpouring thus far of the Jesus Movement, which has revived interest in fundamentalist Christianity among young people across the country."[2]

The festival also represented a widespread shift in conservative churches across the country. Many pastors had decried rock music, long hair, and casual dress . . . anything that seemed like the threatening, chaotic culture beyond the sedate confines of their churches. Chuck Smith and other pastors who had welcomed hippies and opened their churches to fresh ways to praise God had been, perhaps, in the minority. Some conservative pastors without enough to do picketed Explo, pointing out long hair and questionable dress among the attendees, even as the kids inside the stadium earnestly studied their Bibles and attended workshops like "How to Live with Your Parents."

But Explo '72 was a turning point. Billy Graham's presence reassured most of the old guard, and those who attended still get tears in their eyes when they talk about their experience there. Its climax was an unforgettable scene in the Cotton Bowl, the entire stadium swathed in darkness. On stage, Billy Graham and Bill Bright lit candles and then passed the light on to others' candles, which in turn lit others, and others, all through the stadium, until there were nearly one hundred thousand points of light in the darkness, shining individually yet as one. The entire stadium was illuminated with an orange glow. Local residents were calling the Dallas fire department to report that the Cotton Bowl was on fire. They were right: those who attended never forgot the fire of the Holy Spirit and the sense of what Jesus was doing in their world of 1972. Many went on to full-time Christian service.

"When you find out you're not alone, it gives you that much more confidence," a Cru staff person named Bob said later. "You pray different, you act different, you lead different. It was intended to have momentum, and it did."[3]

19

The Church of Stone

The man who will not act until he knows all will never act at all.

Jim Elliot

The church fellowship that a young Greg Laurie started in Riverside, California, in 1972 would eventually become one of the largest churches in America. No one was more surprised than Greg that something like this would occur.

Back in '72, Greg had no idea, really, what he was doing. Today he likes to point out that this was long before churches hired consultants, did branding studies for carefully chosen names, conducted market research of geographical areas, and orchestrated sophisticated social media packages.

It began when the leaders of an Episcopalian church in Riverside, California, got in touch with Chuck Smith and his team at Calvary Chapel. They had heard of the Jesus Movement and wanted something like it to blow through their church. They suggested a Monday night youth-oriented meeting, if someone from Calvary Chapel could come to Riverside to lead it. Their facility was a beautiful, old, traditional stone church, and unfortunately, its numbers were dwindling.

Chuck sent God's secret weapon, Lonnie Frisbee, to the Riverside church . . . and soon the Monday night meetings exploded with three hundred kids, with new converts showing up each week.

At the time, Greg wasn't on staff with Calvary Chapel. He just hung around, willing to do whatever jobs popped up. He'd go see sick people in the hospital. He'd help out with vacation Bible school for the neighborhood children. He'd lead the Bible study in the local mental institution.

On his first visit to that facility, Greg was standing in the lobby with his buddy and fellow hippie preacher, Mike MacIntosh. One of the residents approached them, his eyes a little vacant.

Mike, overflowing with earnest fervor, asked the patient if he had ever met Jesus.

"No," the man responded, brightening up. He stuck his hand out to Greg. "Pleased to meet you, sir!"

The Bible study in Riverside continued to be a "happening" under Lonnie. But then, to Greg's surprise, Lonnie suddenly left Calvary Chapel to join a spiritual movement in Florida.

After Lonnie's departure, the growing fellowship in Riverside began to falter and shrink. Various pastors from Calvary Chapel would take it for one week at a time, but it was an inconvenient drive from Costa Mesa, as the freeways were often backed up with traffic.

One day Greg was hanging out at a staff meeting, and no one else was able—or wanted—to do the Riverside service.

Then they all stopped and looked at Greg . . . eager Greg, at least ten years younger than the rest of the group. He'd do anything. He was like the little brother to whom you could give your smooshed peanut butter sandwich or the chore you didn't want.

"Hey, Greg! Why don't you go down to Riverside?" they asked.

"Yes!" said Greg. He was out the door with his battered Bible before they could change their minds.

Greg arrived in his sputtering Corvair at the address he'd been given in Riverside. It was a stately, traditional, old stone Episcopal church. It looked formal. Greg smoothed his jeans for a moment and then strode in the front door, his Bible under his arm.

An older man was waiting, looking for the pastor from Calvary Chapel who was going to lead the service. "Hello," he said to Greg. "The service won't start for a while. You can wait in a pew until the preacher shows up."

"I've been sent from Calvary Chapel to teach tonight," nineteen-year-old Greg said earnestly.

The older man raised his eyebrows. He waited around for a while. Kids started arriving for the service. And sure enough, no proper preacher arrived.

"Okay," said the church person. "You can speak, but just this one time."

It was not a huge vote of confidence. But Greg wasn't really into a performance mentality. All he knew was there was power in the Word of God, that God had done a miracle in his life, and that he wanted to pass the gospel on to others.

He began to speak, and something started to happen. He was telling the kids about Peter walking on the water, keeping his eyes on Jesus. And even as he was talking, Greg felt like he *was* Peter. As long as he kept his eyes on Jesus, he'd make it through this talk. And then, a miracle: the kids began to sit up, listen, and get into the lesson. At the end, Greg asked if any of them might want to receive Christ. Six young people came forward to pray with him. They were smiling and full of tears.

After the service, everyone was asking Greg if he'd be back the following week. He told them he wasn't sure, thinking that the church staff did not seem particularly enthusiastic about his presence. Then the older guy who'd reluctantly let Greg speak told him he could come back, but that his leadership there would be a week-to-week thing.

This was not an auspicious beginning for what would one day become a direct outgrowth of Greg's experience of the Jesus Revolution: a rousing megachurch of fifteen thousand people. In God's economy, then and now, small beginnings often lead to greater ends.

Greg continued week by week in his probationary leadership of the little Riverside fellowship. The group grew and grew. He met the church rector, a formal, somewhat remote man who didn't seem particularly connected to his people. He hadn't paid much attention to the growing youth congregation within his church.

But then a local newspaper ran a feature story on the weekly meeting. The journalist described it as a "happening," with every pew filled with eager young people. Since the kids were so hungry for God's Word, Greg had also started a Wednesday night service. He'd drawn some graphics and had printed a little bulletin for the flock. In small print at the top of the left page, it said, "Minister: Greg Laurie." Greg hadn't wanted to use the title "pastor." It felt presumptuous. So, knowing that the title "minister" was interchangeable with the word "servant," he'd used that.

It didn't matter. The rector was not pleased. He told Greg that he should become an Episcopalian youth pastor. Perhaps a few years in seminary—preferably one that was far, far away—would get Greg out of his hair, and things could go back to their arid formality, firmly under his control.

Greg thought and prayed about the older man's idea, but felt no leading to pursue it. As the fellowship continued to grow, the rector told Greg he wanted to address the group. He'd speak on topics that he thought were hip and relevant, quoting from *Jesus Christ Superstar* more than the New Testament. To his surprise, the young people didn't really resonate. As young Cathe put it at the time, "We'd all been out there in the world. We didn't want Broadway shows or quotes from the Desiderata or this older guy trying to be cool to relate with kids. We wanted meat from the pure Word of God! It was like food for us."

The rector could not help but notice the cool reception his "teaching" received. Soon a carload of the Episcopal church leaders made its way to Costa Mesa for a meeting with Pastor Chuck Smith. It was time to get rid of Greg Laurie.

Greg, who had seen the angry brothers' arrival, retreated to an empty church office to pray. As he did so, a verse from Psalm 118 kept reverberating in his head: "When hard pressed, I cried to the LORD; he brought me into a spacious place."[1] He didn't know quite what that meant, but he did know enough to call on God in his distress.

The meeting with the disgruntled Episcopalians ended. They jumped in their car and sped away.

The buzzer on the intercom sounded in the office where Greg was praying.

It was Chuck's assistant.

"Greg, Pastor Chuck was wondering if you would come to his office?"

Greg knew that this was the end of his fledgling "pastor" career, and he was back to being simply a starving artist.

"Come in, Greg!" Chuck said cheerfully.

Greg walked hesitantly into the office. Chuck was smiling.

"Greg," said Chuck Smith, "we've got to get you a new church."

20

If You Can Explain It, Then God Didn't Do It

Who gives the keys of a church to a twenty-year-old? Chuck
Smith did.

Greg Laurie

Chuck Smith didn't know just where a new church for Greg
Laurie would be, but he recognized the movement of God
when he saw it. He saw God planting a new congregation
of young people in Riverside. Now it was just a matter of
finding a building for that new church to meet in.

The building came in the form of a Baptist church that had
split, and both of the factions had gone elsewhere. Its former
building was for sale. The former congregants had actually
hauled away their stuff, like pews with brass nameplates
that told who had donated them, memorial hymnbooks, and
chandeliers. The pulpit was still there, but the scene looked
like something from a war zone.

It did not look like the "spacious place" Greg had read about in Psalm 118.

Chuck Smith set up a meeting with the realtor, who was ecstatic that someone was actually interested in the shell of a building. As Chuck and the realtor huddled, Greg walked through the bombed-out sanctuary, thinking about the warring Baptists, the cold Episcopalians, and the fledgling congregation of new believers who just wanted to hear the Word of God. He was twenty years old. He'd been a Christian for three years. He knew God was calling him to preach and teach. But was this how churches started?

Still, Greg had read the book of Acts. He'd seen how the original Jesus Movement moved. His faith was in God, not in a marketing or branding campaign, not in a media platform, not in church growth techniques. He was ready to do what God called him to do, whatever it was.

Chuck was shaking hands with the realtor. He pulled out his checkbook, wrote a check, handed it to the agent, and grinned at Greg.

"Well, Greg," he said. "You've got yourself a church."

Chuck had made the deposit and the first payment for month number one. The rest would be up to Greg and the congregation of young people from the weekly Bible study. None of them had any money besides what they spent on gas and goulash.

Greg made an appointment with the Episcopal rector and told him that he need not worry, Greg was going to move. God had already been building up a new church—a body of believers—and now they had a new building they could meet in.

The rector looked at Greg over his half glasses. "You're going to fail," he said reassuringly. "The only reason all those kids come to the Bible study is because their parents know there are adults here to chaperone them. They won't let their kids come if it's just a big gathering of young people."

Greg thought briefly about breaking the guy's glasses, but decided that would be unbiblical. "All right," he told the older man. "I respect your opinion. We'll just have to see what God does!"

The next week, during the last gathering at the old stone church, Greg announced that the Bible study would be moving to a new location the following weekend. Three hundred excited people were crammed into the church, and they erupted into spontaneous applause.

All that week, Greg had a split screen in his head. On one hand he was trusting God, didn't care about outcomes or numbers, and was ready to speak to however few people came to church, no problem. On the other side he was terrified that no one would show up and *he'd* be shown up as a total failure.

The following Sunday, more than five hundred people arrived to the humble, former war-zone church. To Greg's shock, the rector was one of them. To Greg's further shock, God moved him to have the priest stand before the new congregation as Greg publicly thanked him for his role in getting the new congregation started. Greg didn't elaborate as to what that role had been. Everyone applauded.

The oldest person in the congregation was in his late twenties. There was one child, and so his parents were in charge of Sunday school.

Soon a godly, middle-aged man named Keith Ritter became part of the fellowship. Greg had told the teenagers and converted hippies that they wanted to have "an outreach to older people" on Sunday mornings. That meant people over the age of thirty. Wearing a tie and looking the part of an "older person," Keith preached on Sunday mornings, and Greg preached on Sunday and Wednesday evenings. The fellowship soon had one thousand people, then two thousand in the evening meetings.

But the Sunday morning gathering was staying quite small. In spite of encouragement for him to take it on, Greg felt hesitant. He felt that older people could relate better to Keith than to a youngster in his early twenties who looked like an early cast member of *Duck Dynasty*.

Then Keith had a heart attack. Thankfully, he survived, but he needed to cut back on his schedule. The people in the congregation were already calling Greg pastor. So evidently it was time to step up, even though Greg felt vastly unqualified, and unworthy, to stand in the pulpit.

But for those who were watching, it seemed like God was bringing Greg along step by step. Since his early experience of leading people to Christ in Pirate's Cove, he had wanted to be an evangelist. But he needed the tempering, accountability, and week-in, week-out work that comes with pastoring a flock of people through the ups and downs in their lives. And this fledgling congregation, which needed a pastor, had chosen Greg. He believed in the centrality of the local church, that it was Jesus's designated way to fulfill the Great Commission and bring the love of the kingdom of God to bear on neighborhoods, communities, and nations. And, bottom line, he was really starting to love the people who were part of that church family that would become Harvest Christian Fellowship.

The Jesus Revolution had broken through the structures and strictures of previous, more formal times. In certain areas—like Southern California—the movement was almost a democratization of church life. The cultural model of earlier times had put a premium on a pastor with advanced degrees and a model family, a pillar in the community at large who was as comfortable in the country club or the Rotary Club as in the pulpit. Greg, like many of his young contemporaries of the day, was just amazed he was part of the Jesus Club, where membership was free and all were welcome.

Within a year of getting started, the new church had outgrown its building, and so it was meeting in Riverside's downtown civic center, the Municipal Auditorium. The facility had no air conditioning, and during the sweltering inland summers the faithful would roast like ducks. They called it the "Riverside Municipal Microwave Oven," in honor of that brand-new technology of the day.

The sweaty flock kept growing week by week. Greg couldn't explain why. But, as Warren Wiersbe used to say, quoting former Youth for Christ president Bob Cook, "If you can explain what's going on, God didn't do it."[1]

The other key development in Greg's life that he could not explain was the fact that he was in love with Cathe Martin and wanted to marry her. Coming from the wreckage of his mother's many relationships and the emotional frigidity of his early life, Greg was absolutely amazed that God was giving him something so different. He wanted to grow old with Cathe and to serve God, together, as long as God gave them breath. He wanted to raise children and establish a warm, loving, safe home for all kinds of people in need. He wanted to be part of something he never had as a kid.

That was scary, but Greg had already seen God do miracles. So he was confident that he and Cathe could, with the help of the Holy Spirit, build something strong and healthy and enduring.

Cathe's parents, however, were not so sure. They came from a very different background. They'd lived in affluence all over the world. They wanted Cathe to be provided for, and they were worried that the sins of Greg's mother would somehow be visited upon her son.

So Cathe sat down and wrote her father a long, impassioned letter, trying to show him the new foundation that had changed Greg's trajectory and that would undergird their marriage. She and her dad were living in the same house, of course, but she felt like she could communicate more clearly, and he would pause to really consider her words, if she wrote out her thoughts.

"I love and respect you, Daddy," she wrote, "and I understand your fears for me. But Greg is not his mother. He's a different person." She went on to say how God had changed Greg and was continuing to do so. He was blessing the roast duck church in Riverside—Cathe didn't call it that in the letter—and soon, Greg would even have a regular paycheck of some kind.

Cathe asked for her dad's blessing. She mailed the letter and then crept around the house for a day or two.

As was typical, her dad did not respond outright. But her mother came to Cathe and hugged her tight.

"Honey, your dad got your letter," she said. "It was beautiful. We will give you our blessing."

Greg bought a wedding ring from a friend who'd bought it and then been jilted. So the price was right. And on February 2, 1974—two days after Cathe's eighteenth birthday—Greg and Cathe were married. Calvary pastor Tom Stipe served as best man, and his wife, Maryellen, was Cathe's matron of honor. Cathe wore her mother's beautiful vintage wedding dress. Greg chose a gray tux with wide lapels, a frilly shirt, and pointy, shiny shoes that looked like they'd been purchased at Pimps 'R' Us.

Still, Chuck Smith, who performed the ceremony, was like a proud father. He beamed through the entire proceedings, probably amazed as he contemplated all that God had done in Greg's life over the few short years since he'd first met the seventeen-year-old new Christian brought into the fold by Lonnie Frisbee. Uncharacteristically, Chuck got a little flustered. When he came to the culmination of the service, he paused and then affirmed, "I now pronounce Greg and *Laurie* man and wife!"

Greg and Laurie—we mean Cathe—moved into a creaky old home in Riverside that had been a commune. Another couple lived upstairs. People had given them furniture, like the old green sofa from an earlier century that spewed feathers onto their floor. Cathe sewed her own clothes by hand since she had no sewing machine. She'd been raised in lovely homes around the world, with servants to care for her every need. Now, as mistress of their hippie castle, it was a new world. The first time they received a bill in the mail, Cathe looked at it like it was an artifact from outer space.

"Wow!" she said, shaking her head. "You mean you have to *pay* for water?"

Yes, they did have to pay for water, but when Cathe became pregnant, they found an obstetrician who would deliver their baby for free. Actually, Cathe was working for the doctor, so he donated his services to deliver baby Christopher, who arrived fourteen months after they were married.

Christopher was an enthusiastic, inquisitive, energetic only child for ten years, and then Jonathan arrived. He was as easygoing as Christopher was irrepressible. Sometimes, watching his boys play outside with Cathe, Greg would feel overwhelmed. As the son of a serial divorcée, he never could have dreamed he would have a fruitful, faithful, enduring marriage. As a fatherless boy, he never could have dreamed he would get to be a father to two beautiful sons.

Still, he didn't know then that they would break his heart.

21

Hippie Preachers

I admired their complete contentment, with nothing of the material realm. All they needed was a box of raisins and some oats and they were ready to minister for God anywhere they were called. It was so beautiful, their simplicity of faith and trust in Jesus.

Chuck Smith, reflecting on hippies
who came to know Christ

Greg Laurie was but one of a crop of young men who met Christ during the Jesus Movement in Southern California and then went on to start growing, vital churches. This was in 1974, before the boom of casual worship, seeker-friendly churches, and many of the outreach innovations that are common today. Back then contemporary Christian music was in its infancy, and casual dress was still a new development in many sanctuaries.

But even though these new churches were contemporary in style, their pastors didn't try to make the gospel more relevant by modifying its message. The young preachers stuck to the basic proclamation of the Bible that had evangelized and discipled them. They did what they had seen Chuck Smith do. They didn't pursue trendy topics; they taught, verse by verse, through entire books of the Bible.

Greg's church was overflowing with young people who were coming to church for the first time in their lives, excited about following Jesus. These kids were bringing their parents with them. The church grew. They expanded to three overflowing services on Sunday mornings, and two on Sunday evenings. A flourishing "Through the Bible" study met on Wednesday evenings.

Greg surrounded himself with people God was calling to minister in the same way, people he felt were smarter and more gifted than he was. In the beginning, they were brothers like Bob Probert, Paul Havsgaard, Fred Farley, and Duane Crumb. Later, John Collins, Jeff Lasseigne, Ron Case, Paul Eaton, and Brad Ormonde would join him, along with many other gifted colleagues over the years. He knew ministry was a team effort, not a one-man show, and he had seen what happened to pastors and leaders who had no accountability in their lives. They blew off course. And since he came from an early family life with little structure and lots of deception, he wanted to build a ministry with strong foundations and honest communications. He knew it wouldn't be perfect—but even at a young age, he had the wisdom to design the new church with strong accountability in place.

As the church grew, Greg and his team launched a daily radio program, calling it *Harvest Celebration*. They recorded it in a friend's bathroom because they thought the acoustics were better there. Greg had a drawing board set up in his office and was still doing all kinds of graphic design to support himself, as he had no real salary. They put out tracts designed to tell people about Christ. Eventually they got access to television programs and big public events where Greg would preach an evangelistic message and give people the opportunity to publicly come forward and receive Jesus. These updated Billy Graham–style events were called Harvest Crusades.

At this point, Calvary Chapels were popping up everywhere in Southern California, and sometimes people would get mixed up as to which church was which. Greg's fellowship in Riverside was becoming better known for the "Harvest" name because of the outreaches. So while their theology and philosophy were the same as their original Calvary Chapel roots, they officially became Harvest Christian Fellowship. Today they are affiliated with the Southern Baptist Convention.

While Greg was cultivating the Harvest church, other hippie brothers were starting new congregations as well. These organic outreaches to the places the brothers had come from started as Bible studies, and then swelled naturally into new congregations.

Jeff Johnson was a great example. Jeff had been a surfing, opium-smoking hippie in the late '60s. He'd searched for truth in Buddhism, Hinduism, Hare Krishna, yoga, and hypnosis. He dealt drugs on his home turf of Downey, California. When he came to know Christ at Calvary Chapel, he wanted to start teaching the Bible to the guys to whom he had been dealing drugs. Calvary Chapel in Downey started in a park; within five years, it was meeting in a facility as big as six football fields. Today the church has about eight thousand members, an adoption ministry, radio and mission outreaches, and Christian schools.

Mike MacIntosh was a poster child of the early Calvary Chapel days. His mind had been so damaged by drugs that he once turned himself in to law enforcement, telling police that he was the "fifth Beatle" and he'd lost part of his brain. He ended up in an Orange County psychiatric ward. Then one night in 1970, he came to faith in Jesus at Calvary Chapel in Costa Mesa. He grew in a solid understanding of God's Word. God restored his broken marriage. He became a pastor and went on to start Horizon Christian Fellowship in San Diego. It began as a home Bible study of twelve people, grew into a megachurch, and has planted more than thirty additional congregations.

Raul Ries had grown up in the tumultuous heart of urban LA. He was a fierce street fighter and kung fu expert who served in Vietnam. He received two Purple Hearts for bravery, but the war fueled the rage that filled his heart. Raul came home, married, and had children, but his fury corroded everything in his life. One night, gun in hand, he decided to end it all . . . but as God would have it, the television was on, and there was Pastor Chuck Smith, being interviewed about the Jesus Movement. Raul listened, and only the Holy Spirit could have orchestrated what came next: he surrendered his life to Jesus, right there in front of the TV.

God changed Raul's life and restored his marriage. Raul started a church—where else?—in his kung fu studio. Today that little congregation has about thirteen thousand people; they no longer meet in the studio. Raul has a thriving ministry all over Southern California and far beyond.

A guy named Joe Focht came to Christ in Southern California and later moved to the East Coast. There he started a Bible study with twenty people. It became Calvary Chapel of Philadelphia, with more than ten thousand adults, and four thousand children enrolled in its Sunday school ministry. It's planted twenty more churches in the Delaware Valley area.

Skip Heitzig grew up in a religious home in Southern California but sought his spirituality in drugs and the occult. One day in 1973 he gave his heart to Jesus Christ while watching a Billy Graham crusade on TV. He studied the Bible for eight years under Chuck Smith and then moved to Albuquerque, New Mexico. In 1982, he and his wife began a home Bible study, which grew into Calvary Chapel Albuquerque. Within six years it was, for a time, the fastest growing church in America. Today about fifteen thousand people attend each week, and the congregation has planted churches in Arizona, Colorado, and other parts of New Mexico.

Don McClure grew up thinking he was a Christian because, after all, "everyone born in America was a Christian." But when he was a junior in college, while at a Billy Graham crusade in Los Angeles, he made a decision to follow Jesus. He went on to Bible school, then seminary, and served as Chuck Smith's assistant pastor for four years. Then he and his wife moved to Lake Arrowhead, where they planted a church, a Bible college, and a conference center before they moved on to plant churches in other areas. Today they teach at conferences, retreats, Bible colleges, intern programs, church services, and "any other door God opens," as they put it.[1]

Steve Mays took the drug-addled prototype of rebellious '60s youth to new heights. In high school he would take twenty dextroamphetamine tablets, crush them, add an Excedrin and a vitamin—for good health—and swallow it all with coffee. One evening his parents came home and found that he had wedged the front door shut with towels; when they crashed through it, a wave of water came gushing out. Steve had made the living room into a gigantic indoor bathtub and was sitting in the middle of it, smoking a pencil and laughing at a television show. The only problem was that the TV was not turned on.

The next day, as the house—and Steve—were drying out, Steve's dad noted his son making two sandwiches and pouring two glasses of milk for lunch. When his dad asked who the other sandwich was for, Steve earnestly told him that it was for Brad, who lived in the clock on the wall.

Leaving Brad and his parents behind, Steve went on to darker adventures. He got involved with gangs and crime. One day he was literally lying in the gutter when a couple named Shirley and Henry picked him up. They were Christians. They took Steve in, gave him a shower, and fed him. Then they told him about Mansion Messiah, one of the Christian communes that had grown out of Calvary Chapel in Costa Mesa. According to Steve, the rest of the story came down something like this:

"I walked in [to Mansion Messiah] with my gun stuck in the back of my pants. Immediately, this little squirt named Orville looked right in my eyes and said, 'Do you know Jesus?' And I said no."

Steve prayed with the squirt to receive Christ. "God just grabbed me, reached in and burned in my heart," he said later. "It was the most incredible power I have ever experienced in my life. . . . At that moment God delivered me from drugs. I flushed ten thousand dollars' worth of drugs down the toilet that day. I also threw my gun away in the ocean. The residents of Mansion Messiah buried my clothes, they smelled so bad. From then on, I started singing Christian songs by myself when I was just walking down the street."[2]

Steve went on to learn the gospel, study the Word, and become the lead pastor at Calvary Chapel South Bay, just south of Los Angeles, in 1980. The church started with seventy-five members, and Steve served as its leader for thirty-four years, until he died unexpectedly during back surgery in 2014.

Today, the little church started by the once-hopeless drug addict is a mission-minded, diverse, and flourishing congregation of more than eight thousand people.

So for Greg Laurie and his fellow hippie preachers, the decades that followed the excitement of the Jesus Movement were in fact a season of joyful but hard work: planting, cultivating, and shepherding new groups of Christians. These were new *ekklesia*, gatherings of believers that created an environment similar to Chuck Smith's church where many of the hippie pastors had been born again. The brothers' new churches evangelized, discipled, served, and grew over the years . . . and so did Greg's.

One day many years ago, when Harvest Christian Fellowship had reached around eight thousand in Sunday attendance, Greg took a phone call from a person at an organization that specialized in megachurches. At the time, Greg didn't even know what a megachurch was. But the guy told him that Harvest Christian Fellowship, the little church that no one wanted back in 1972, was at that point one of the largest churches in the United States.

22

Malaise and the Me Decade

To live for the moment is the prevailing passion—to live for yourself, not for your predecessors or posterity. We are fast losing the sense of historical continuity, the sense of belonging to a succession of generations originating in the past and stretching into the future.

Christopher Lasch, "The Narcissistic Society"

The Jesus Revolution was primarily a youth movement. It exploded with great vigor and fervor, and as its people got older, its dramatic presence in the American consciousness gently faded away. The young Jesus converts like Greg Laurie grew up. They settled down, married, and began having children. They started churches, careers, and ministries. Some went to the mission field, either in the US or in faraway places. Some went into politics or business or the law. Some became priests. Some wrote books, recorded albums, had reunions, and laughed when they looked at old photos of their hippie days. It was a new season.

The broader culture of the baby boomers changed as well. The revolutionary fervor and energy that had characterized the '60s shifted to a more cynical, less activist status quo. Two enormously different events shaped this transition. They were very different, but at the most fundamental level they shared the same dark root: humankind's insatiable hunger to gain and retain power, regardless of the cost.

The first is the specter that grew in the '50s and '60s, convulsed in the '70s, and has haunted America ever since. The Vietnam War.

The second is the scandal that began with a third-rate political burglary at a Washington office complex and became a cover-up that toppled a president. Watergate.

The '70s were surely shaped by other events as well. In May 1970, National Guard troops killed four students during an antiwar protest at Kent State University. In 1971 the first microprocessor computer chips were developed. In the winter and spring of 1972, President Nixon made historic and unprecedented trips to China and Moscow. That fall he won a landslide reelection to the presidency.

In January 1973, the Supreme Court ruled in *Roe v. Wade* that a woman could not be prevented by her state from having an abortion in the first six months of pregnancy. That same month the Watergate burglars were convicted, and presidential aides started bailing out, one by one, to reveal a massive cover-up at the highest levels of government. The nation became aware of a White House taping system whose big reel-to-reel tapes had relentlessly recorded the conversations that had shaped history.

For example, Richard Nixon told a speechwriter in 1968 that he had "come to the conclusion that there's no way to win the war" in Vietnam. He continued, "But we can't say that, of course. In fact, we have to seem to say the opposite, just to keep some degree of bargaining leverage."[1] The war would go on spilling certain blood for uncertain reasons for five more years, until the US pulled its last troops out of Vietnam in 1973.

After the start of the Arab-Israeli War in October 1973, oil imports from Arab nations were banned in the US, creating an energy crisis. In May of '74, impeachment hearings began against President Nixon in the House Judiciary Committee. On August 9, 1974, Richard Nixon resigned the office of the presidency. Vice President Gerald Ford was sworn in as president. No doubt wishing he was playing golf somewhere in a land far, far away, one of his first official acts was to pardon Nixon in an effort to spare the nation the ongoing pain of a long, ugly trial.

In April 1975, a guy named Bill Gates and his buddy Paul Allen started a little company; they called it Microsoft.

At the end of that month, North Vietnamese forces completed their takeover of South Vietnam as American embassy staff hurriedly abandoned Saigon. The communist regime's blood-red flag with its yellow star flew over the former capital, now renamed Ho Chi Minh City.

President Ford survived two assassination attempts, one by former Manson Family devotee Squeaky Fromm, who showed up with a gun a few feet away from the president at a Sacramento event. (She later explained that she had wanted to make a statement against environmental pollution and its effects on air, trees, water, and animals. Fortunately for Mr. Ford, her pistol jammed.)

In late 1975, a guy named Gary Dahl began selling egg-sized stones, nestled in straw, in cardboard boxes complete with air holes. Pet Rocks were an immediate sensation and made Dahl a millionaire. The *New York Times* later opined, "The concept of a 'pet' that required no actual work and no real commitment resonated with the self-indulgent '70s, and before long a cultural phenomenon was born."[2]

By 1976, two geniuses named Steve created the first Apple desktop computer. Steve Jobs sold his VW Microbus to finance their venture; Steve Wozniak sold his calculator. The wood-cased, hand-built personal computer was the new Apple company's first product. Jimmy Carter was elected president. Bolstered by Carter's outspoken faith and the 1976 conversion autobiography of one of Nixon's most notorious henchmen, Chuck Colson, "born again" became a familiar term in the public lexicon. *Newsweek* magazine proclaimed 1976 "The Year of the Evangelical"; its cover story made no mention of the Jesus Movement. America celebrated her bicentennial.

As the '70s wound down, a movie called *Star Wars* became the top-grossing film of its time. President Carter presided over the Camp David peace agreement between Israel and Egypt. The first Polish pope, John Paul II, was elected. He would play a key role in the collapse of communism in the former Soviet Union. In 1977, *Saturday Night Fever* hit movie screens, celebrating the last popular music movement that was driven by the baby boomer generation: disco.

In the fall of 1978, more than nine hundred members of a "rainbow family of equality" followed the instructions of their malevolent leader, Jim Jones, and killed themselves with cyanide-laced Kool-Aid in their commune in Guyana. The Three Mile Island nuclear power plant had a partial core meltdown, fanning fears of environmental disaster.

Sixty-three Americans were among ninety hostages taken at the American embassy in Iran by radical followers of the Ayatollah Khomeini, who had deposed America's former ally, the Shah of Iran. By the summer of '79, the nation was preoccupied with yet another oil crisis, long gas lines, habitual disillusionment, and a brand-new fear—Islamic fundamentalism.

For those who lived through the '70s, these factoids create a dot-to-dot narrative where memories fill in the blanks. For those who didn't, it's a *Forrest Gump*–style survey of a time long gone.

Vietnam tore up a generation. Its prisoners of war came home with tales of hard-core patriotism and faith that pulled them through their long days and terrible nights in captivity. They and other vets were met with jeers, insults, and derision. People called them "baby-killers." Popular films released in the late '70s, such as *The Deer Hunter* and *Apocalypse Now*, showed the misery, evil, moral ambiguity, and horrors of the war in a way that shocked armchair Americans. More than fifty-eight thousand American service members died in the war, their names now engraved on a long black wall of stone in Washington, DC. Hundreds of thousands of other young men and women were physically and psychologically wounded. The war created a widespread, powerful tide of betrayal, shame, mourning, waste, suspicion, and deep, deep sadness.

The gradual reveal that was Watergate, so soon after Vietnam, augmented the effect, generating a perfect storm. If US presidents from Kennedy through Nixon had deceived Americans about the war in Vietnam, now Nixon's profanity-filled tirades, neuroses, and lies created a profound, weary distrust and malaise in America.

Historians like to point to one speech by President Jimmy Carter that spoke to the prevailing mood of the late '70s. It's known as "the Malaise Speech," though Carter never used that depressing word in it. Speaking from the White House in July 1979, Mr. Carter earnestly told Americans:

> I want to talk to you right now about a fundamental threat to American democracy. . . . It is a crisis of confidence. It is a crisis that strikes at the very heart and soul and spirit of our national will. We can see this crisis in the growing doubt about the meaning of our own lives and in the loss of a unity of purpose for our nation. . . .
>
> In a nation that was proud of hard work, strong families, close-knit communities, and our faith in God, too many of us now tend to worship self-indulgence and consumption. Human identity is no longer defined by what one does, but by what one owns. But we've discovered that owning things and consuming things does not satisfy our longing for meaning.[3]

Mr. Carter went on to expand on the pressing issue of the moment, the energy crisis caused by turmoil in the Middle East. He asked Americans to use public transportation or carpools to save fuel, to turn down their thermostats, and to obey the speed limit.

But it's unlikely those energy-saving tips would in fact create a new strength in America. The crisis Carter identified went deeper than the cost of gas. It wasn't just a crisis of confidence. It was a deeper crisis of cynicism.

The mood was very different from the revolutionary tone of the '60s. Chaotic as they are, revolutions are expressions of hope. They are fueled by the belief that change can happen and that it will bring a desired result.

The tone of the late '70s was less idealistic and less hopeful. It lacked the generous, group-oriented spirit of the '60s. It was far more focused on the self than the community. President Carter's speech warned:

> We are at a turning point in our history. There are two paths to choose. One is a path I've warned about tonight, the path that leads to fragmentation and self-interest. Down that road lies a mistaken idea of freedom, the right to grasp for ourselves some advantage over others. That path would be one of constant conflict between narrow interests ending in chaos and immobility. It is a certain route to failure.[4]

A few years before President Carter's speech, the celebrated cultural commentator Tom Wolfe made his own analysis of the decade in an article in *New York* magazine. Wolfe profiled the '70s as a movement away from the communitarianism of the hippie movement and toward a new celebration of the individual. He called the new time period in which America found herself "the Me Decade." The pendulum of history had swung from the antimaterialistic, communal revolution of the flower people to a more consumer-centered, individualistic, selfie default that seems to have reigned ever since.

The Me Decade marched onward into the 1980s, the 1990s, and the new millennium of the post–9/11 world. America saw the rise of the Moral Majority and other faith-based movements of evangelical involvement in politics. Ronald Reagan ambled into the White House. The Soviet Union collapsed and the Cold War came to an end. The economy boomed, as did Christian parachurch ministries, movements like Promise Keepers, and new, growing megachurches all over the United States. As always, there were ample political and sexual scandals, and the rather spectacular downfalls of soiled televangelist empires. The stock market soared, crashed, and soared again. Progressive social movements unleashed in the '60s grew in their mainstream power. Wars and rumors of wars tore up the Middle East, Africa, Asia, and elsewhere. True racial and ethnic reconciliation was still a dream. Drugs continued to destroy the lives of countless young people. Characters as disparate as Bushes, Clintons, Obamas, and Trumps occupied the White House. And still, as Sonny and Cher sang in 1967, the beat goes on.

Back in 1979, Pastor Chuck Smith reflected on life, history, and all he had seen God do in the Jesus Revolution. He wrote a book called *End Times*. He wrote that he believed the world could end by 1981. He acknowledged he could well be wrong.

He was.

But still, one era was ending in America, and a different world was emerging.

23

Tea or Revolution?

Everywhere the apostle Paul went, there was either a riot or a revival. Everywhere I go, they serve tea.

An Anglican bishop

Like the New Testament itself, the Jesus Movement had a wide cast of characters. They were wonderful, weird, damaged, powerful, prophetic, and everything in between. The Holy Spirit works in all kinds of strange and surprising ways. His effects can't be graphed. His movements can't be dissected; they are alive. Jesus saved souls, rescued people from drug addiction, planted lonely people in families, revived churches, and changed human lives. Some people walked with Him for a while and then fell back into old ways. And over the years, perhaps some of His former firebrands were more likely to be found at home sipping tea, so to speak, than preaching Jesus on the streets.

One person who probably never stayed home sipping tea was Lonnie Frisbee. Abundantly gifted and deeply wounded,

Lonnie was a restless soul. His journey took him from the Southern California Jesus scene in the early '70s when he got involved with a pyramid style of leadership and cell group "accountability" called the Shepherding Movement. Like any human endeavor, it was subject to excess and abuse; Lonnie later said that "the heavy-handed 'shepherding' experience almost did me in. It did do me in . . . and it was also a disaster."[1]

He surfaced again in Southern California in 1980. Chuck Smith had invited him back to Calvary Chapel, but to Greg Laurie, it seemed like Lonnie was trying to recapture the former glories of his early Jesus Revolution days. A paid newspaper advertisement featured a photo of him as the man who started the Jesus Movement. It seemed odd for Lonnie to take credit for something Jesus had done. And when Lonnie would speak, chaos would sometimes ensue. One Calvary Chapel staff member was surprised when Lonnie addressed a youth group meeting in May 1980 and kids started falling on the floor like trees in a forest, crashing into chairs, some speaking in tongues, some crying and confused because of the chaos.

Other times when Lonnie would appear at churches or other gatherings, he wasn't as winsome as he once had been. His humor seemed angry and brittle. Some said that he felt cut out of the history of the Calvary Chapel movement, or that he hadn't been compensated fairly for his service while there. He and his wife had divorced in 1973; she said it was because of an extramarital affair on her part.[2] Lonnie later called it a "dirty, disgusting, gutter relationship of adultery," though he said he later baptized the man and that God bonded them in the love of Jesus.[3]

Back in their early days, Greg had felt that as long as Lonnie was around Chuck and his systematic teaching of Scripture, he seemed to do well. But while Chuck's church services focused on love as the key manifestation of the Holy Spirit in modern times, Lonnie was more interested in intense signs, wonders, healings, and current-day Pentecostal miracles. Because of his "Jesus" look in the booming days of Calvary Chapel in Costa Mesa, many newspapers and magazines had heralded him. He was a favorite on the popular television program of Kathryn Kuhlman, a vivacious personality who held charismatic healing services.

After leaving Calvary Chapel a second time, Lonnie traveled the world, preaching with John Wimber. John was a gifted Calvary Chapel pastor who had eventually shifted much of his emphasis from evangelism and discipleship to dramatic and demonstrative manifestations of the power of the Holy Spirit, and founded the Vineyard Movement. Lonnie and John would conduct "healing clinics." Lonnie once described a series of gatherings in South Africa where "in every single one of the meetings the warts were dropping off people's hands . . . instantaneously gone. Big warts . . . to them it's nothing, because they have witch doctors, wart witch doctors in Africa and you could go to that witch doctor and he does a little thing and throws smoke in the air, gives you something and the warts are supposed to fall off and sometimes they do."[4]

In other meetings, both in the US and abroad, there was often chaos as people fainted or shrieked in unknown languages, heralding Lonnie as a miracle worker. To Greg, Lonnie's preoccupation with physical manifestations and experiences seemed a long way from preaching the gospel and giving glory to Jesus.

Meanwhile, Lonnie had slid into an undercover homosexual lifestyle, and he eventually contracted AIDS. This was early in the disease's development and treatment in the US, and there were no lifesaving options available. Sadly, by early 1993 he was terminal.

Greg and his old friend Mike MacIntosh went to visit Lonnie in early March of '93. He was in hospice care in Newport Beach.

They were met by a caretaker who guided them up some stairs to a wide room. Lonnie was on a couch, in obvious pain. He was like a skeleton with skin, but that made his smile all the bigger as he welcomed his old friends. He reminisced about old times, but also told them how he knew he would be miraculously healed and would continue his preaching ministry to big crowds around the world.

At the same time, though, he told them he was sad about the course his life had taken. He said he regretted some of the choices he'd made.

The sun set, and Lonnie's caregiver lit a fire in the fireplace. Lonnie kept talking, his face lit by the warm flames. The sight took Greg back to the old days at the retreats in the mountains more than twenty years earlier. They had all been so young then. They'd build a big fire, and Lonnie would preach to all the Jesus People while the flames danced and the logs crackled. Greg and Cathe, and so many others, had been so proud and thankful that he was their preacher.

But now it all felt so different to Greg.

The fire was so small, and Lonnie seemed smaller too, like a young boy. His life was flickering out. Mike and Greg hugged him carefully so as not to hurt him, told him they loved him and they'd see him in Heaven, and then they all prayed together.

Lonnie Frisbee died a few days later, on March 12, 1993. He was forty-three years old.

————

Throughout the '90s and into the new millennium, Greg pressed on with Harvest Christian Fellowship, its evangelistic crusades, a daily radio program, television opportunities, and a growing internet presence as social media exploded and technology allowed for powerful new ways to spread the gospel. He served on Billy Graham's board of directors and grew in his friendship with the revered preacher. Dr. Graham would send him sermons, and Greg would give him ideas for current illustrations to support his points. During crusades, Greg would be in the arena, listening to Billy Graham preach. He never lost the thrill when he'd hear his hero use his material. And he loved that when they'd have dinner or just talk, Billy Graham didn't drop names about all the world leaders and celebrities he knew. He didn't hold forth with his own stories as much as ask his companions about *their* stories. Greg respected his integrity, his humility, and his lifelong commitment to evangelism, to the glory of God. He was, like Jesus, as gracious to the person he met on the street or in a restaurant as he was to a president or a celebrity. Billy Graham wasn't perfect, but he was a great role model.

As time went by, it was clear that Greg's hair and his youth might be gone, but he still had that absolute passion for souls that God had created in him from his beginning "sermon" at Pirate's Cove in 1970.

Like most of us, though, it turned out that the toughest people for Greg to evangelize were his own family. He had what was basically a full-time ministry trying to share the gospel with his mother's flock of ex-husbands. He did enjoy a sweet, miraculous relationship with Oscar Laurie, Charlene's husband who had adopted Greg as a child and given him his name. Later, Greg had the surreal opportunity to meet his birth father. It was an absolutely underwhelming experience. And at the end of her long, restless life, Greg's mom, Charlene, came to know Jesus before she died.

Members of every generation need to find Jesus on their own, and sometimes kids react against those who have come before. Greg's grandparents had been Christians, set in their legalistic ways. Greg's mother rebelled against them and ran away from faith. Greg saw the futility of his mom's alcohol-muddled existence and eventually ran the other way, toward Jesus. Then, for a time, his own kids chose the habits of this world and a double lifestyle.

It's not uncommon for pastors' kids to feel the fishbowl pressure of other people's expectations. Many revolt for a while against the boundaries and behaviors that have been part of their world for as long as they can remember.

It killed Greg and made him half-crazy with fear to see his older son Christopher wander into drug use as a teenager and young adult. On the one hand he was still the charming, handsome, beloved son, and on the other hand he was a full-blown prodigal, far from God.

Sometimes he wouldn't show up for a commitment, and Greg would drive over to his apartment and pull him out of bed.

Chris would bat the air and head back to the covers.

"Just leave me alone, Dad!"

Greg's heart would break. "I will not leave you alone!" he'd tell his son. "I love you. I would do anything to save you. You cannot live like this!"

One morning Greg couldn't find Christopher. His then-girlfriend didn't know where he was. Neither did any of his other friends. He wasn't picking up his phone calls. All Greg could envision was his son dead in a ditch somewhere. He called a friend who was a police officer and asked him to check everywhere that he could.

Greg paced, his stomach in a knot. The phone rang.

"Are you sitting down?" his cop friend asked. "He's in the Santa Ana Jail. He got pulled over last night and was arrested for drugs. Possession of Ecstasy."

Greg exhaled. At least Christopher wasn't dead. At least he hadn't killed someone in a car wreck.

But then his heart fell. He thought back to his own bad trips as a teenager on LSD. And now here was his son doing the hallucinogenic thing. Why?

Christopher probably couldn't have really answered that question at the time. And maybe the question wasn't so much why he was running away from Jesus but when he would turn back to Him. Like all of us, he had to come to that turning point on his own. Only the Holy Spirit could break through to his wandering heart.

It happened one day in the shower. As Christopher told his mother later, he was standing under the stream of water, feeling it flood over his face, and was crying out to God about the mess he was making of his life.

"Help me!" he cried. "Show me what to do!"

By the end of the shower, two things had happened. Christopher had decided to marry his girlfriend, Brittany. And, in the words of the old Jesus People song, he had decided to follow Jesus. *No turning back.*

They were married in 2006. Christopher had been working at a local design firm as a graphic artist, but as he became more involved with church life again, he switched over to working at Harvest in Riverside. He loved using his artistic gifts for the glory of God. He and Brittany had a baby daughter, Stella. They were building a little family, a new life, and had just opened their home to a weekly Bible study. Life was sweet.

Jonathan Laurie, ten years younger than his charismatic older brother, had a totally different personality from Christopher. He didn't gravitate to the spotlight. He wasn't the life of the party. He was more of an observer. He'd graduated high school and worked a series of jobs. Greg, feeling like Jonathan needed to settle down and get a work ethic going—just as Greg had years earlier under Chuck Smith—helped his son get a job as a metal finisher at a friend's aerospace firm. Jonathan was working hard, coating aircraft parts and sweating all day long. He was living at home to save money. But like his brother before him, he was juggling a double life. Dope on Saturdays—well, dope *every* day—and church on Sundays. Sipping coffee and chatting at the sunny breakfast bar with Mom and Dad, with pornography and alcohol and drugs stashed in dark corners in his room upstairs. He was miserable, but he hid it all pretty well. His parents didn't even know what he was doing.

By 2008, Greg and Cathe sensed that Jonathan was drifting, but beyond that they were hopeful that he, like Christopher, would soon come to the point of being totally sold out to Jesus.

Otherwise things were going well. Harvest Christian Fellowship was humming along like a well-oiled machine, with great people in place, exciting programs, and ongoing growth. Greg was speaking to hundreds of thousands of people at a time at stadium events that had their origins in the old Billy Graham crusades of the past generation, but tooled for current ears. Same gospel, new hearers.

Once Greg and Cathe had adjusted to the strange reality that they just weren't twentysomethings anymore, they had gone crazy about being grandparents. Two-year-old Stella called them Papa and Nama. It was magical. And Christopher and Brittany were expecting a second baby daughter in the fall.

Greg's memoir from that year, *Lost Boy*, traced his dysfunctional past to God's incredible blessings on his life. It ended with joyful family photos, and looked like all it needed was the tagline "and they lived happily ever after."

It was a season of peaceful maintenance, of continuing to cultivate fields that had been plowed long ago. Greg felt overwhelmed with gratitude. Given his lonely childhood and fractured teen years, now he felt rich in the things he'd once thought he'd never know: a real relationship with God. An intact, lifelong marriage. A loving family. Solid work in a community of faith, a broader family of Christian brothers and sisters. When he was young he had felt like he was drifting in a vast wasteland, and now it was all a miracle, like God had made his life into a beautiful, blooming garden.

What Greg didn't know was that his garden was about to get plowed under, and God was about to upend his life in a stark, new, very personal Jesus Revolution.

24

Burning It Down

O my son! My son, my son! If only I had died instead of
you—O my son!

King David

"Where are you?"

It was about 10:00 a.m. on July 24, 2008. Greg was texting
his son, Christopher, again, even though he'd just called him.
Cathe had called Christopher as well; so had Brittany, his
wife. All Brittany knew was that Christopher had left their
home in Orange County at his usual time, and headed on
the 91 freeway on his way to work at the Harvest church in
Riverside. His station wagon was loaded with flats of water
bottles, soft drinks, and other supplies for their two-year-old
daughter's birthday party that weekend. He was running a
little bit late.

That Thursday morning, Cathe was leading a Bible study
with Brittany and her mother, Sheryll. They were both new

believers, and had been meeting weekly with Cathe for a couple of months, discussing the book of Philippians.

Greg was upstairs babysitting toddler Stella. They were playing on the floor with blocks, but Greg was preoccupied.

Where was his son?

Then he and Cathe started getting phone calls, but not from Christopher. From people at church telling them to just stay put. It was confusing. And ominous.

Thirty-five miles away, eastbound drivers on the 91 freeway honked their horns and strained to peer past the endless lines of cars in front of them. The rush-hour traffic, always heavy, was at a standstill. Sirens wailed as police cars and rescue vehicles tried to make their way toward the epicenter of the chaos. Helicopters spun low as traffic reporters relayed the news: there had been a terrible accident. A Dodge Magnum station wagon moving at a high rate of speed had rear-ended a slow-moving state highway truck clearing debris from the carpool lane in Corona. Smoke rose over the sweltering, gridlocked freeway.

One of the first responders to the crash scene found the driver's license of the car's sole occupant, and he recognized the last name of the victim. The emergency worker called the Harvest church . . . and now the only thing that Greg and Cathe knew was that some of their closest friends, the other pastors from the church in Riverside, were on their way to the Lauries' home in Newport Beach.

Brittany called the California Highway Patrol, asking if there had been an accident on the 91 freeway. Maybe Christopher had just gotten caught in a huge traffic jam on his way to work. Brittany was put on hold. Then the dispatcher clicked back on and asked her to describe her husband's car. When he heard her say it was a Dodge Magnum station wagon, all he told her was that yes, there had been an accident.

Still, the little group at Greg's house hoped. Maybe he was just injured. Maybe it wasn't what they feared. Maybe things would be okay.

Brittany grabbed her purse and headed out the front door; she said she had to drive to the freeway, now, and find her husband. Greg and the others rushed out with her, trying to stop her from driving when she was so distraught. Then they all saw a car approach and glide next to the curb in front of the house. It was the pastors from Riverside. They parked and walked slowly toward the porch.

Pastor Jeff Lasseigne led the way. His eyes filled with tears. He gently took Brittany's arm, and then he managed one short sentence: "Christopher is with the Lord."

In his catastrophic collision with the thirty-thousand-pound highway maintenance truck, Christopher had suffered devastating injuries to his head and chest. He had died instantly.

Greg fell in a crumpled heap on the porch, weeping. Cathe fell with him, her arms around him. Brittany was vomiting into the bushes as her mother tried to hold and steady her.

Devastation.

The next few days kaleidoscoped into a blur of old memories and breaking waves of fresh pain. Brittany's health and pregnancy were the major concern. No one could sleep or eat or process the fact that Christopher—husband, father, brother, friend, son—was so abruptly gone.

Greg and Cathe wept, hugged, read Scripture out loud, prayed, and cried some more.

The days that followed were months long. Christopher's funeral. Huge church services full of truth, tears, and praise to the God who walks with the grieving through the valley of the shadow. And sadly, because of the Lauries' public profile, there was a lot of media coverage of Christopher's death. It brought a new level of pain.

Reporters researched details about Christopher's life that no one would want exposed on the front pages of a newspaper. They published parts of his driving record, which was less than pristine. They reported that Christopher had committed a felony: possession of Ecstasy, a controlled substance.

Bloggers got into the act, spewing hate. Greg made the mistake of reading their comments. The kinder ones blamed Christopher for his own death, said they were glad he died, and called him a privileged idiot, part of a hypocritical religious empire.

Greg felt like he'd been shot, then stabbed over and over and over.

As Greg grieved, he talked with a close friend, Jon Courson. Jon had lost his wife in a car accident when his children were very young; then, when his oldest daughter was sixteen, she too was killed in a car crash. Jon had been through the deep valley of the shadow. He knew the crushing grief of sudden loss.

"I'll never have another son," Greg told his old friend. "Brittany will eventually have a new husband; she's young, and life will go on. But I'll never have a new Christopher."

"That's true," Jon told him. "But you *will* have a new Jonathan."

He went on to say how Jonathan had always been in Christopher's shadow, like a younger tree under a big oak. Now the Lord had removed the big tree . . . and Jonathan was going to flourish.

On the day of Christopher's death, twenty-three-year-old Jonathan Laurie arrived home from work soon after his parents and sister-in-law had been told of his brother's passing. A leader from the church had come to his office and told him what had happened. He was in a fog. He kept running his hands through his long blond hair, shaking his head. All he could hear in his mind was Christopher's voice.

"When are you going to quit the double life?" he'd asked Jonathan. "When are you going to stop partying and come back to your faith? What's it going to take?"

Jonathan knew his older brother was right. He thought of all the times he'd tried to stop drinking and smoking dope. He'd throw his stash out of the car window, resolving never to use again. The next day he'd be out in the street looking for the baggie he'd tossed. It might have been run over by a car, crushed and dirty, but he'd still use it. Like a dog going back to its vomit. Day after day after day. He was so tired and disgusted. But he could not stop.

The night before Christopher's death, Jonathan had been out with friends, doing the party thing. On his blurry way home, he thought—again—about how miserable he really was.

Tomorrow, he thought. *Tomorrow after I get off work, I'll go talk with Christopher about all this.*

Now it was tomorrow. And his brother was gone.

"What's it going to take?"

Evidently, it had taken Christopher's death.

Jonathan sat on his bed in his room, looking at pictures of his brother. He wept. Then he tore through the room, grabbing up all the drugs he'd hidden there, all the paraphernalia, the porn, and other stuff. He made a pile on the bed and got on his knees.

"God," he said. "I am so sorry! You know that I've proven to You and myself that I'm incapable of doing this on my own. I can't stop using this stuff in my own strength, so You're going to have to help me. But I want to follow You and serve You for the rest of my life, however long that is."

Jonathan would go on to a new life, his own Jesus Revolution, really. It started with repentance and a tearing down of the old. Then God built him up new. Jonathan married and had a family. He began to work at Harvest, doing anything he could to help build up the fellowship there. He'd heard the Bible all his life, but now he found that he could not study the Word of God enough; it was like he had a brand-new hunger for truth, at all costs. He began to teach small groups and meet with people who were struggling with their faith. His quiet steadiness was a comfort to many. And to his own surprise, like his father before him, people spontaneously began to call him "Pastor."

Even as he celebrated the "new" Jonathan, Greg still grieved the loss of his older son. He often saw a montage of pictures in his head, seasons over the course of Christopher's life. Some had been hard. But all of it, Greg knew, had been under the big umbrella of God's grace.

Greg remembered six-year-old Christopher riding the waves on his miniature surfboard, his eyes huge at the sight of the surf. Christopher building towns made of LEGOs and coloring endless pages of drawings. Christopher playing on the floor with his GI Joe aircraft carrier, landing little jets on its plastic deck. Greg thought of the hard times, of rousing his son from a druggy sleep or pulling him out of some stupid bar.

And he thought of his son getting baptized in the Sea of Galilee just two months earlier during a church trip to Israel.

Greg and the other Harvest pastors had been baptizing new believers one by one by one, and Christopher had been shooting photographs. Then, out of the corner of his eye, Greg saw Christopher hand his camera to someone else and wade over to Greg's colleague, Pastor Jeff Lasseigne.

"I want to be baptized," Christopher had told Jeff. He'd felt like since he had truly surrendered everything to Christ, he wanted to make a public affirmation that he had decided to follow Jesus for the rest of his life.

No one had known, of course, how short a time that would be.

"Buried in the likeness of Christ's death," Pastor Jeff had said back then, grinning as he put his arm around Christopher and dunked him into the ancient waters of the Sea of Galilee.

Then he had lifted him up, the sunlight shining on Christopher's streaming head and the huge smile on his shining face.

"And raised in the likeness of His resurrection!"

25

Muscle Memory

I need God. I just *need* God. It's hard. When this happened, if Jesus didn't come through for me, trust me when I tell you that I would have stopped preaching, but I have to say to you, it's all true. I hit bottom and God was there. And this horror brought good things. If I could have all the faith, urgency, passion, abandon that came—if I could have all that—*and* Christopher, it would be a perfect world. For me, I had personal revival through it.

Greg Laurie

It is doubtful whether God can bless a man greatly until He has hurt him deeply.

A. W. Tozer

The second that Greg Laurie heard his son was dead, he prayed a prayer.

"God," he said, even as he was collapsed on his front porch, weeping. "You gave him to me in the first place, and now I give him back to You."

It was no heroic, super-spiritual moment. It was just the culmination of years of consuming the Bible. Like a soldier who drills for so long that his performance on the field of battle comes automatically, or the athlete who practices until her muscles have a memory of their own . . . at the moment of crisis, faith was a net that caught him, and it held.

Greg kept thinking of the book of Job—how many times had he preached on Job? In a series of painful disasters, God takes everything, material and personal, away from Job. Job falls on the ground in worship, and cries out, "Naked I came from my mother's womb, and naked I will depart. The LORD gave and the LORD has taken away; may the name of the LORD be praised."[1]

Greg had no choice, of course, regarding his son's death. It happened. But in the aftermath, he did have a choice. On the one hand, he could sort of paint by numbers with a fake, superficial religiosity, and give up and drift for the rest of his life. On the other, he could go back to the bedrock, to the absolutes of his faith, and vigorously trust God for whatever new thing He was now doing. The Jesus Revolution that had turned Greg's life upside down back in 1970 *had* to be real and powerful almost forty years later.

It was.

But the reality of faith didn't anesthetize the pain. Trusting Jesus wasn't an emotional Xanax. Greg and Cathe hurt all the time, their chests pressed with a constant, crushing weight. But faith did make it bearable, second by second by second.

And because they had studied the Bible, day in and day out, for years, they knew a few things. Not just intellectually, but deep in their souls, things they could hold on to in the midst of the storm.

First, they knew that life is full of trouble, just as Jesus had promised. Greg realized that he had unconsciously assumed that because his childhood was so full of pain, he might get a break as an adult. Not so. But the pain of this world made Heaven itself much more real, and now they found they were thinking of Heaven all the time, with great expectation.

Second, they knew God loved them.

Third, they knew that Jesus wept with them.

Fourth, they knew that God can be glorified, in some mysterious way, by human suffering.

These plain and dependable truths were amplified and supported by their community of faith. Though there will always be people who say ridiculous, hurtful things in times of bereavement—"Are you over it yet?"—they were in the minority. The Lauries' church family, and the wider body of Christ, prayed for them, wept with them, listened to them, fed them, hugged them, and hung with them for the long run.

So the Lauries found that the faith they'd first found as hippie teenagers was still absolutely reliable in the perilous world of middle-aged loss. But they also found they were in a new revolution, one of coming back to the fixed point at which they'd started. Jesus. Everything else in their familiar landscape, with its unconscious assumption that things would proceed in a certain, safe way, was gone. Burned down like a forest fire. Nothing was left of the familiar except the foundations of faith, like the bones of the earth.

In some ways the Lauries felt what C. S. Lewis had expressed about the death of his beloved mother when he was a child: "With my mother's death all settled happiness . . . disappeared from my life. There was to be much fun, many pleasures, many stabs of joy; but no more of the old security. It was sea and islands now; the great continent had sunk like Atlantis."[2]

Storms will come. Fires will burn. Terrorists and rogue governments will attack. Stock markets will crash. Cancer and other disease, accidents, murder, suicide, betrayal, and death—they *will* come in this world. For Greg, in the fulcrum days after the loss of his son, life came down, oddly enough, to the same essential question that Lonnie Frisbee had posed to him when he was seventeen years old.

"Are you for Christ, or against Him?"

Except now the question was, "Do you trust Christ, *really*, or don't you?"

When fires and floods come, you don't mess with the small stuff. You grab on to what is most important. However much time Greg might have left in his own life journey, he didn't want to coast. He wanted to trust Christ, take risks, and be bold. Eternity was a second away. This wasn't the time to retire to Hawaii and collect seashells, or to show up on Sundays at his megachurch and dust off an archived sermon he'd written ten years earlier. This wasn't the time to let down his guard against the enemy and have an affair, or turn to a little or a lot of social drinking, or to fall into bitterness. This was the time to gamble it all, to live as if he radically trusted Christ. Or not. It wasn't like Greg had strayed; but it was time to make sure that he was doing the first things.

Not too many megachurch pastors start over. It's too risky. Greg Laurie did.

For a long time he'd loved Orange County. It was where he'd lived for years, even though his big church was in Riverside. It was where Greg had grown up, come to Christ, and seen the Jesus Movement burst out like a flame. It was time to come back home and plant a church. It was time to return to the first things, to take the principles he'd first seen in the Jesus Movement and do the basics. After all, they say if you want to see a revival, do revival-like things.

He'd stayed away from Orange County for years because of Chuck Smith's big church there, the very first Calvary Chapel. But there were plenty of unsaved people in Orange County, and Greg felt a growing conviction that God was in fact calling him to start a Bible study there. Out of respect, Greg called his old mentor and asked for his blessing on this new venture. Chuck enthusiastically told Greg that, as always, he was behind him.

When the time came to launch, however, Chuck had cooled to the idea. He'd told other people that he was not happy about Greg's new venture. He saw it as competition. Even when Greg met with him to talk further, Chuck was adamant, and Greg was less than successful in ironing out the tension between them.

He was determined to resolve the painful conflict with Chuck, but he knew it would take time. And in the aftermath of tragedy and his own new sense of urgency about the gospel, Greg wasn't going to wait around. It would have been far easier to pull the plug on the new venture of faith to keep peace between him and Smith, but Greg could not deny the strong leading of the Holy Spirit to do this work.

He and Cathe were also concerned about Christopher's wife, Brittany, and her mother, Sheryll. They wanted to continue their discipleship, but they were fragile. So the senior Lauries decided to start a Thursday night Bible study in Orange County, with the intention of helping to root Brittany and Sheryll deeper in the Scriptures that alone could anchor them. If others wanted to listen in for the study, so much the better.

Greg looked around for a venue. It was hard to find a church that wanted Greg Laurie to teach a Bible study there. It was like the stone Episcopal church in Riverside more than thirty years earlier. But back then the pastor thought Greg was too young and inexperienced to possibly shepherd a flock. Now it seemed like area pastors didn't want to host "celebrity pastor" Greg teaching a study because he was a threat to their own flock. But then the leader of the Free Chapel in Irvine, Jentezen Franklin, opened up his large space for Greg and Cathe on Thursday nights. "This may turn into a church," Greg told him. "No problem," Jentezen said. He told Greg it was his privilege to help Greg fulfill what the Lord was calling him to in this new season of his life.

On the first Thursday, Cathe and Greg showed up well ahead of time. They brought worship leaders from their church in Riverside. Cathe and her closest friends, Marilyn, Shelly, and Sue, baked dozens and dozens of peanut butter and chocolate chip cookies. They brought khaki tablecloths and draped round tables in the foyer. They brought glass cylinder vases from home, filled them with long, curly willow twigs, and hung lanterns from the branches. At the end of the service, they stood behind their festive tables, dispensing cookies and welcoming people.

A thousand people showed up. The next week there were more. And more each following week. Cathe and her faithful friends had to supplement their baking capacity with bulk purchases from Costco, but they kept it up for the first year.

But Greg purposely did not sprinkle Miracle-Gro on this new fellowship. He didn't do splashy advertising or bring in big Christian bands that would draw a crowd. He didn't prime the pump with anything besides cookies and the Word of God, taught simply, verse by verse by verse. He'd always told younger pastors that your people will develop an appetite for what you feed them, and now he was trying to keep it simple and pure.

He did find that his pain had had some benefits. He was more open with people about his own personal struggles. He judged other people's life situations less. He moved toward suffering people rather than away from them. He took the time to connect.

It was kind of like being a grandparent, he thought. When you're young and raising your children, it all goes so fast. When you're a grandparent, you slow down and enjoy it. When Greg was young and starting his church, everything was new, the church was growing, and he was just trying to keep up. He had wanted to be successful, and he hadn't wanted the numbers to diminish.

Now he could take it slower and enjoy the relationships. He wanted to know the people. It was a different dynamic. At his Riverside church, he'd be in the greenroom backstage, or passing quickly through a crowd with security around him, necessary because of frequent threats against his life. Now he was talking with people after the services, eating tacos from a food truck in the parking lot with everyone else.

Security was still around, but at a distance so people could more easily approach him.

Now, instead of seeing a blur of faces, he saw people, and he knew their stories. Oh, that couple who had been struggling in their marriage, now they are mending, sitting together, holding hands. That single mom who was at the end of her rope, now she has a community. That teenaged kid who was strung out on drugs, now he's clean and sober. Greg loved seeing people come to Christ, grow in maturity, discover their gifts, and serve God with passion and joy.

For her part, Cathe and her closest friends knew that women's ministry would be the nucleus of this new church. Women, as always, set the tone. Women's ministry at Harvest had never been emotionally based in the first place, but Cathe had seen other big churches where women's events had a fluffy, feel-good focus or a lite menu of games, fashion shows, and skits. Cathe had experienced how the Scripture itself had sustained her in her deepest grief of losing her firstborn son. She wanted the women of Orange County to digest the strong meat of the Word of God together and to develop close friendships with like-minded sisters who could walk one another through the storms of life with love and grace.

So week by week, Harvest Orange County grew. Soon they added Sunday morning services to the Thursday evening Bible studies. They outgrew their borrowed building. They found a former graphic design studio that was properly cool and funky and actually had dozens of surfboards already hanging from the ceiling, thrown in for free. The Southern California vibe was perfect.

Starting up Orange County not only revived Greg and Cathe but it also injected fresh life back into their megachurch in Riverside. Returning to the essentials and doing the "first things" is not only for start-ups; it's the only way to grow deeper and stronger for the long haul.

Still, the damaged relationship with Chuck Smith was painful. Greg wanted to repair it. When he was young, there were so many broken parts of his childhood, so he became a fixer. If his mother was drunk and passed out again, he'd take care of her. If he was the new kid in school yet again, he'd make friends. If his mom's current husband was mean, he'd retreat to his own private world.

Now, as Greg thought about Chuck, he felt like he owed him a huge debt. It helped him to think of Chuck back when he was younger, how Chuck had loved people, opened the doors to his church, and sought God's will in some pretty radical ways. Greg thought that actually, Chuck, on his worst day, was better than most people on their best day. He thought of how Chuck had taught him so much as a young person, and how he'd given him the keys to his first church when Greg was a twenty-year-old nobody.

Chuck had lost his brother and his father in a small plane crash when he was younger. Now, in Greg's loss of his son, he thought that maybe Chuck had sealed off parts of himself, years ago, from relationships. He'd been a competitive, hard-driving, hardworking kind of guy. Greg remembered once pointing out to Chuck how many young men he'd inspired to go into ministry. "It's not a big thing," Chuck had said. "I just teach the Word of God in such a simple way that they think, 'Oh, I can do that too!'"

In January of 2012, Greg invited Chuck to come to the Harvest church in Orange County. Just before the event, Chuck discovered that he had lung cancer; he would have surgery the following week. Two thousand people gathered to hear the old pastor and his protégé reflect on the Jesus Movement.

Greg and Chuck talked about the colorful days in the early 1970s when Chuck bucked convention and opened his church to barefoot hippies. Greg told people how Chuck had opened the doors for what became contemporary Christian music and worship. He described how Chuck's "emphasis on Bible exposition not only changed a church, it changed a generation, because thousands of young men, now not so young, went out around the country and around the world and started Calvary Chapel–style churches . . . more than 1,400 around the world today."[3]

Greg told the people how Chuck had asked him to do an outdoor event at an Orange County concert venue back in 1990. This grew into Harvest Crusades . . . which, at the time of their conversation in 2012, had reached 4,400,000 people with the gospel, and 370,000 of them had made commitments to follow Jesus.

Greg asked Chuck to share counsel for hard times. "Don't give up," the veteran pastor told the crowd. "Never trade what you do know for what you don't know because [when tragedies strike] the question is always, 'Why?' That question will haunt you and make you crazy. . . . I don't know why. But what I do know is that God is good and God loves me and God is working on His perfect plan in my life. So, I'm just content with that."[4]

Greg asked his old mentor about Calvary Chapel. How had it served as a place where the Jesus Movement could flourish, back in the day?

The church had been built, Chuck said plainly, on the Bible. Nothing fancy or trendy. "It is the exposition of the

Word of God. It's encouraging people to read the Word of God and expounding to them the Word of God. . . . It's just God honoring His Word, as He said He would."[5]

A year or so later, Greg went to see Chuck preach at Calvary Chapel Costa Mesa. He thought of the great memories he had of that place, and all that this man had taught him and done for him. Chuck was in a wheelchair, and before the service Greg went to him and knelt by his side.

"Chuck," he said, "I wanted to come and say hello, and tell you that I love you."

Chuck turned to Greg and grinned his big old grin. "I love you too!"

After that, Chuck was rolled onto the stage, and some fellow pastors lifted him onto his stool so he could preach. He had a canister of oxygen next to him, and tubes running into his nose . . . and then Chuck opened and taught publicly from the Word of God one last time.

Chuck Smith died on October 3, 2013.

His funeral was held at the eighteen-thousand-seat Honda Center in Anaheim. Every seat was filled, with another fifty thousand people watching around the world. Asked by Chuck's son-in-law to give the message that day, Greg paid a final, loving tribute to the man who gave him a chance when no one else would.

26

Desperate Enough?

Till sin be bitter, Christ will not be sweet.

Thomas Watson,
The Doctrine of Repentance

Years before Chuck died, Greg asked him if he thought there could be another Jesus Revolution.

"I don't know," said Chuck. "Back in the '60s, people were desperate. Unsaved people were spiritually hungry. They were searching for God. I was desperate, too: desperate to be part of what God was doing. So I guess the question for today is, 'Are we desperate enough?'"

Many Christians today yearn for revival. Whether in big events like the National Day of Prayer, or small prayer meetings in rural chapels, inner cities, college campuses, or suburban fellowship groups, believers are pleading with God to revive His church and send spiritual awakening to our land. Seminary students and laypeople are reflecting on those unusual times when God's Spirit did wild things in America's history.

Chaos and desperation are far more likely to lead to revival than comfort and complacency. That's true in the celebrated revivals and awakenings of America's past.

The First Great Awakening started shaking the American colonies in the late 1730s, a fairly secular time period when Enlightenment thinking had made many colonists skeptical of biblical Christianity. It began in New England, where a thirty-seven-year-old preacher, Jonathan Edwards, was earnestly praying for conversions in his staid congregation in Northampton, Massachusetts.

Sunday by Sunday, people started coming to faith in Jesus. Over time, this trickle became a torrent, most notably when Edwards was asked to fill in for a pastor in a neighboring congregation in sophisticated Enfield. His sermon, "Sinners in the Hands of an Angry God," is regarded today as a classic "hellfire and brimstone" address. People think of this sermon as an agitated harangue in which Edwards angrily whipped his poor listeners into a frenzy.

In reality, Edwards stood solemnly at the pulpit, hunched over the tiny writing on the wrinkled pages of his thick manuscript. He read his sermon in a monotone, glancing up occasionally to contemplate the back wall of the church.

But then something strange happened. The pure power of the Word of God—Edwards' text was in Deuteronomy—did something extraordinary. The men and women in the pews shook and wept, crying out with moans and shrieks. They knelt on the cold floors. In despair over their sins, they repented, committed themselves to God, and joined the tide of the Great Awakening.

Edwards went on to become the second president of Princeton University and is considered one of the greatest intellects of the American pre-Revolutionary period.

But the Great Awakening did not stem from Edwards, gifted though he was. Nor did it flow from the great outdoor preaching of George Whitefield, who told the gospel story all over the barns, riverbanks, and fields of America, drawing huge crowds and becoming one of the most well-known men in America at that time. The Great Awakening came about purely by the will of God and the power of His Holy Spirit.

As Edwards put it, the collapsing people who came under conviction were experiencing "an extraordinary sense of the awful majesty, greatness and holiness of God, so as sometimes to overwhelm soul and body, a sense of the piercing, all seeing eye of God so as to sometimes take away bodily strength."[1]

Paradoxically, and wonderfully, the *fear* of God also caused these repentant souls to revel in a new, joyful *love* for Him. They "felt a great delight in singing praises to God and Jesus Christ, and longing that this present life may be as it were one continued song of praise to God."[2]

Between twenty-five thousand and fifty thousand of these new converts flooded into New England's churches . . . out of a total population in the region of three hundred and forty thousand people.

The awakening faded, as all revivals do. Within fifty years, interest in Christianity had been superseded by preoccupation with this world. As America expanded to the Wild West, many towns, saloons, and frontier settlements had a law unto themselves, and God wasn't so much a part of its enforcement. Outlaws and desperados created havoc. Then a Second

Great Awakening began near the turn of the nineteenth century, when revival meetings in Kentucky, Tennessee, and Ohio spread like wildfire among different denominations.

Crowds of as many as fifteen thousand people would gather for several days for camp meetings to hear circuit riders preach. Thousands of people on the frontier heard the gospel, repented, and started living for Jesus. In the eastern part of the country, a young lawyer in his thirties, Charles Finney, grew to prominence. Finney was a former skeptic who'd been converted; he became an aggressive itinerant evangelist whose preaching drew throngs to faith in Jesus.

A third awakening is known as the Fulton Street Revival of 1857. The mid-1800s had been a period of financial expansion. Gold had been discovered out West, railroads were booming, and industry and commerce were riding high. Generally speaking, spiritual interest was low. But a tall, forty-eight-year-old former businessman named Jeremiah Lanphier hungered for people to come to Christ. He initiated a weekly prayer meeting, from 12:00 to 1:00 p.m., on the third floor of an old church building on Fulton Street in New York City.

At noon on September 23, 1857, Lanphier sat alone in the drafty room and waited for somebody—anybody—to join him. Eventually, over the grindingly slow course of the hour, five other men did. They prayed. The group felt no great outpouring of God's Spirit. They determined to meet again the following week.

Twenty men came to the second meeting, and forty to the third. Then, on October 14, the stock market crashed. There was financial panic. Banks closed. Men lost their jobs and homes. Families were hungry. People were desperate. Soon three thousand men and women were crowding Lanphier's prayer gatherings, now meeting every day and in locations all over New York, filling theaters on Broadway.

Within six months, ten thousand people gathered daily for prayer throughout New York City. Prayer meetings spread to Chicago, where two thousand people showed up to petition God for souls in the Metropolitan Theater. They spread to Washington, DC, to towns across the Midwest, to the West Coast, and into Canada and beyond. For two years, God used this nonsectarian, laypeople's movement in a revival of prayer that brought tens of thousands of new believers and reinvigorated Christians into churches all over the country.

Awakenings and revivals tend to get their own boldface titles in history books and websites. The Jesus Movement gets mixed reviews.

Some historians call the Jesus Movement an awakening and revival because of its scope: thousands of young people were saved all over the United States, and thousands of Christians were refreshed and revived in local churches.

Other commentators who look for cultural consequences of revivals say that the Jesus Movement was a revival because it led to the election in 1976 of Jimmy Carter, the "born again" president, and the rise of the Moral Majority in the '80s, contributing to an upswing of evangelicalism that has "prospered" ever since. Such analysis seems to equate political access or social popularity with spiritual influence, something that would no doubt surprise the writers of the New Testament.

Other historians dismiss the Jesus Movement as just a cultural blip on the spiritual radar, no big deal.

Perhaps the discussion of whether the Jesus Movement was a "true" awakening or revival is a debate best left to academic circles. For his part, Greg believes it was the last great American spiritual awakening, and he passionately hopes for another, if God would be so gracious, in his lifetime.

However we define the Jesus Revolution, it is clear that God's Spirit spontaneously stirred in unusual ways among unusual people during the hippie era. We will not know until we see with the scope of eternity what darkness and evil at work in the world was constrained by those conversions, or what ripple effects those transformed lives brought to generations to come.

Take Greg, for example. This kid who came to Christ in the Jesus Movement has seen five hundred thousand people make what he calls "professions of faith" in his Harvest Crusades. Hundreds of thousands more have come to faith through his nearly fifty years of gospel preaching at his church and through radio, TV, and other venues. It would not be an overstatement to say that more than a million people have prayed with Greg to follow Jesus. It just goes to show that God can use anyone who truly decides he or she is "for Jesus," as Greg did in 1970, to accomplish extraordinary things for His kingdom.

The Jesus Movement awakened many, many dead souls. Most of them had at least one thing in common: they were desperate. They'd sought peace, love, and community in the utopian visions of the day. They'd thought that drugs would bring spiritual enlightenment, or that sex would bring love, or that music would bring community, or that all those things would bring freedom. They had been disappointed by the counterfeits and were hungry for what was real. It was no casual thing when they discovered in Jesus the reality they'd been looking for.

These new converts were on fire. Their long hair was standing on end. They preached on the streets. They hitchhiked solely for the purpose of sharing the gospel with people who'd pick them up. They lived together very simply. They started storefront missions. They fed hungry hippies. They believed that the Bible was true, that Jesus was the Savior of the world He loved, and that He was coming again very soon. They depended on the power of the Holy Spirit. Their numbers multiplied.

Over time, what started as a spontaneous movement of the Holy Spirit among these flower children became more mainstream. The spiritual awakening among the unsaved became a revival among the saved. It wasn't just an alteration in the trimmings of many churches and parachurch gatherings, like adopting casual dress or contemporary music, though those changes did happen. It was a deep hunger for the Bible itself, for prayer, fellowship, evangelism, and discipleship.

It was not humanly orchestrated. Revival doesn't start with church consultants, though consultants can help churches be better stewards of their resources. Revival doesn't start with programs, though programs are wonderful things. To put it in hippie language, Chuck Smith didn't sit down and plan a "happening" back in 1970. (Neither did Jonathan Edwards in 1742.) The Spirit of God started something . . . and Chuck Smith and others recognized it and responded in obedience to what *God* was already doing.

God grants revival. He grants it to those who are humble enough to know they need it, those who have a certain desperate hunger for Him. Only out of self-despair—a helpless understanding of the reality of sin and one's absolute inability to cure it—does anyone ever turn wholeheartedly to God. That desperation is sometimes hard to come by in America, because it is the opposite of self-sufficiency. In the US, many of us live under the illusion that our needs are already met, that maybe God is an add-on to our already comfortable existence.

Poor and persecuted Christians in other parts of the world face horrific challenges in their everyday lives, but they are rich in faith. They *know* that their next breath, their next meal, and their next life are all absolutely dependent on the grace of God. Their desperate reliance on Jesus gives them a strength we often lack in our own muddled affluence. They pity American Christians who don't have the stark luxury of such clear priorities, those who have become like the first-century believers to whom Jesus said, rather radically,

> I know your deeds, that you are neither cold nor hot. I wish you were either one or the other! So, because you are lukewarm—neither hot nor cold—I am about to spit you out of my mouth. You say, "I am rich; I have acquired wealth and do not need a thing." But you do not realize that you are wretched, pitiful, poor, blind and naked. I counsel you to buy from me gold refined in the fire, so you can become rich; and white clothes to wear, so you can cover your shameful nakedness; and salve to put on your eyes, so you can see.[3]

People don't tend to seek God when they are comfortable. Pain and suffering amplify the sound of God's voice; we can become deaf to His call in times when life is easy. Our hearts can close tight, sealed by a heavy, rusty door.

But Jesus loves us. He says, "Here I am! I stand at the door and knock. If anyone hears my voice and opens the door, I will come in and eat with that person, and they with me" (Rev. 3:20).

That image is often used to woo unbelievers to open their heart-doors to Jesus, which is great, but that section of Scripture was of course written to *believers* . . . or at least people who professed to be believers. Their tepid faith was neither cold nor hot, and therefore had all the power and passion of congealed oatmeal.

Thankfully, Jesus says in the same passage, "Those whom I love I rebuke and discipline. So be earnest and repent!"[4]

Distinguished Regent College professor, author, and Jesus follower J. I. Packer has written:

> Much is heard today of spirituality as self-discovery and self-fulfillment in God and of a relationship with God that brings happiness, contentment, satisfaction, and inward peace. But of bearing the cross, battling wrong desires, resisting temptation, mortifying sin, and making those decisions that Jesus pictured as cutting off a limb and plucking out an eye, little or nothing gets said.
>
> Yet this is the living out of repentance, and without realistic emphasis on this more demanding side of the Christian life, a great deal of self-deceived shallowness and a great many false professions of faith from persons ignorant of the cost of discipleship are bound to appear.
>
> *Now it is precisely the life of repentance, of cross-bearing, of holiness under pressure and joy within pain—the life, in other words, of following Jesus on his own stated terms—that God revives* . . . we do well to ask ourselves whether this is something we have come to terms with as of now.[5]

Do Christians today truly *long* for revival and awakening? Are we ready for this "living out of repentance"? There is a cost. It is different for each person and each church community. But for all of us, repentance means that something has to die.

27

Cultural Christianity Is Dead: Rest in Peace

Little by little, the church loses its grip on essential things, becomes a social club, goes to sleep or flies off at a tangent. All over the world we find sleeping churches, and all around them are the gospel-starved masses. Instead of performing the first thing of importance, evangelizing the masses, they are engaged in a bewildering variety of pastimes—anything but the real thing.

J. Edwin Orr

en·cul·tu·ra·tion
noun

"the gradual acquisition of the characteristics and norms of a culture or group by a person, another culture, etc."

Oxford Dictionary of English

In October 1967, when the hard-core hippies of San Francisco's Haight-Ashbury conducted their mock "funeral for the hippie," it wasn't just a groovy happening or a public relations stunt. Hippies weren't much into public relations. The funeral was an ironic rejection of the commercialization that had taken over their once-unadulterated movement. In the beginning, people were coming together to embrace deeply held hippie values. Now it had turned into a circus. Tour buses were canvassing the Haight; middle-aged tourists were snapping photos with their Kodaks and buying hippie gear.

Dismayed by such consumerism, the organizers of the hippie funeral also wanted to dissuade kids who were belatedly looking for the San Francisco experience as their way to climb on the hippie bandwagon.

"We wanted to signal that this was the end of it, to stay where you are, *bring the revolution to where you live*," explained one of the funeral organizers."[1]

It's not a perfect analogy—and it's *only* an analogy—but a half century later, maybe it's time for Christians to conduct a similar funeral. It would be a burial of what we might call enculturated Christianity, a blending of commercial and consumer values with the gospel we once embraced on its own. Maybe it's time to bring the Jesus Revolution back to where we live.

The hippies of '67 packed their fake coffin with trappings like bongs, love beads, and incense. The fake coffins for the funeral of enculturated Christianity would likely have different contents.

Maybe we should have special services and solemnly carry coffins up the aisles of our churches, or place them on the stages of our worship centers, and fill them with all the stuff that we've unconsciously attached to our understanding and practice of Christianity, stuff that is just not part of the gospel. There might be physical things we need to give up, things to which we've become addicted. Maybe there *would* be some bongs, or prescription drugs, or alcohol, or food, or pornography.

But most of the ugly coffin space would be needed for attitudes and habits of the heart. It might be a set of unconscious racial or ethnic prejudices that we've absorbed from our upbringing, biases that have nothing to do with the radical realities that Jesus taught and demonstrated. For others of us it might be the assumption that God helps those who help themselves, and that Christianity is about pulling ourselves up by our own bootstraps to gain position and success—good old American individualism that judges and excludes the weak. It might be a condemning attitude toward outsiders, toward those who are not "Just Like Us." It might be the assumption that God wants us to be materially wealthy, healthy, safe, and comfortable. It might be a long-held assumption that God is a Republican. Or a Democrat. Or an Independent.

The point is, each of us has different idols that subtly come from the culture around us, idols that we spin and polish so we can incorporate them in our nice religious experience. An "idol" is anyone or anything that takes the place of God in our lives. Throwing away such things has been a struggle for believers since the beginning. New believers in ancient times used to bring their household idols and other objects that were part of their pre-Christ life, and cast them into huge bonfires. In rural villages in Asia and Africa, new believers still do the same today. Even in our sophisticated culture—*especially* in our sophisticated culture—the world, the flesh, and the devil get hold of our minds and affections so easily. And the next thing you know, we've figured out a way to accommodate their influence. When that happens, it's time for a new revolution.

What would funerals of enculturated Christianity look like? The answers are as varied as the hundreds of thousands of churches across America. The idea is not meant to be prescriptive; it's simply a question for corporate communities of Christ followers to answer as the Holy Spirit gives conviction. It's certainly no new message that the American way of life has an insidious way of corrupting the purity of our understanding and practice of the gospel.

In the 1950s and '60s, many churches needed to repent of knee-jerk racist attitudes. It's our human tendency to be jerks, so it's no surprise that some of us might need to do the same today.

In Chuck Smith's Costa Mesa church in 1970, his congregants had to bury their prejudice against hippies who looked and smelled different from them. Today that might mean that some of us need to bury our bias against various ethnic groups, migrants, refugees, addicts . . . all kinds of people in need.

There are regions where faith becomes "churchianity," woven with social standing, family heritage, and cultural expectations. There's left- or right-leaning politicized faith of every kind, which blurs and distorts a biblical understanding of the kingdoms of this world and the mysterious and transcendent ways of the kingdom of God.

In some megachurches today, there's been an easy drift toward style over substance, where such accoutrements as smoke machines, slick production values, lattes in the lobby, and sermons designed for short attention spans take precedence over the transformational power of the Word of God. It's devilishly easy for market preferences to shape the message itself, sublimating the radical, absolute, and ancient distinctives that make the church the church. There's also that tendency, in churches both large and small, to seek growth for growth's sake. That can result in the priority of maintaining a building or a complex, so then a certain capital budget must be met at all costs, otherwise known as "feeding the elephant." It's so easy to lower our standards in order to extend our reach.

If we produce consumers instead of communers, we end up with customers instead of disciples. This can create a whole new category of people: evangelized nonbelievers, or people who think they are Christians when they aren't. They've lived in a church that is so accommodating that the gospel is compromised, and people become hardened to the very truth that could transform and revolutionize their lives.

Enculturation is no new threat. It's been the subtle enemy of the church since its beginnings. The apostle Paul pled with the early Christ followers to renounce cultural prejudices, the love of money, sexual accommodations, and the love of power. We need to continue to be diligent two thousand years later, on watch and ever ready to bury the usual suspects.

What's in your coffin?

28

Mere Revival

I continue to dream and pray about a revival of holiness in our day that moves forth in mission and creates authentic community in which each person can be unleashed through the empowerment of the Spirit to fulfill God's creational intentions.

John Wesley

John Wesley dreamed of and prayed for a revival of holiness in his day . . . in the mid-1700s. Whether we're in the eighteenth century, or the first century or the dog days of the twenty-first century, times are hard, and we all need Jesus to revive us.

Still, it's hard to imagine a new Jesus Revolution sweeping America today. We live in a time of great cynicism in the media, crass polarizations in the national political debate, and the lack of civil discourse that once characterized the American experiment. Seventy percent of Americans believe that the country is as divided today as it was during the chaotic era of the Vietnam War. The same percentage says that the nation's politics have reached a dangerous low point, and a majority of those believe the situation is a "new normal" rather than temporary.[1]

This cynicism is no help in a world of violence, terror, uncertainty, corruption, and fear. Reports of terrorism abroad or at home fill our news feeds every week. Sex trafficking and human slavery are the scourge not just of faraway brothels and labor camps but of suburban America. Drugs were not just a threat in the '60s and '70s; today's crises of addiction, narcotics trafficking, and opioid and other epidemics are as grim as ever.

The much-vaunted sexual revolution of the '60s seems quaint in a world where mainstream platforms like Facebook offer four or five dozen different gender options for you to choose from in order to identify yourself. Or you can custom design one if your preference is not on Facebook's list. Redefinitions of marriage, sexuality, and gender itself are pushing for normalization across the board—soon available in preschools near you. Today's celebration of diversity and tolerance tolerates anything except an exclusive truth claim. The Jesus Movement's One Way hand sign—as in there's but one way to Heaven, through faith in Christ—would be derided by some as offensive hate speech today, with Jesus People carted off to jail or to community service and sensitivity training workshops.

Still, let's not get wigged out about culture wars or the increasing marginalization of biblical Christianity. This is a time, like all eras on our planet, of great opportunity. The upheaval actually combines an odd blend of cynicism and longing, ugliness and beauty, despair and hope. And one thing we know: Jesus looks upon our world and loves its people. His holy affection floods toward all, every tribe, nation, individual on this terrestrial ball . . . and He calls those who follow Him to be the visible manifestation of His love and His truth.

That's a challenge we cannot meet without humility, personal and corporate repentance, and the fresh wind and power of His Holy Spirit.

What would a new Jesus Revolution look like today?

All we know is that it would be scary, exhilarating, messy, passionate, and surprising. We should not pray for revival unless we are ready to be turned upside down, our heads and our pockets and our lives shaken out. During times of revival, the transcendent power of God is unleashed in human beings . . . and when the divine is poured into the human, we can expect human beings to act in unusual ways.

A new revival might well start, as did the Jesus Movement, among the least likely people. But whatever God chooses to do, we do know a few things about what happens when revival comes, regardless of its time period or cultural context.[2]

First, God comes down. The weight of His presence is unmistakable. Revival is no human endeavor. It is an electric encounter with the Other—the Eternal One who lives from everlasting to everlasting, the God who is beyond our dimensions—that brings about the conviction of sin. Just as at Pentecost, when the apostle Peter preached and his hearers were "cut to the heart," they responded by asking what they could do to get rid of their guilt. "Repent, then," said Peter, "and turn to God, so that your sins may be wiped out, that times of refreshing may come from the Lord."[3] There is no refreshment without the conviction, confession, and forgiveness of sin.

God's Word pierces human hearts. The teaching and proc-lamation of the Bible itself is central, for revival is a divine synthesis of mind and heart, more than just emotional ex-perience and more than just cognitive assertions.

Lives change. In true revival, there is a wholesale renuncia-tion of sin and its patterns. People live differently than they did before, to say the least.

When all these things happen, there is an unmistakable flood of love that fills the local community of Christians, both new and old. For example, Jonathan Edwards wrote that his colonial "town seemed to be full of the presence of God; it never was so full of love, nor of joy . . . as it was then. There were remarkable tokens of God's presence in almost every house."[4] There was an extravagant outpouring of care, outreach, and generosity that characterized the early New Testament church.

The revival flood also brings love's sister, joy. "Under first-century revival conditions," writes J. I. Packer, "inexpressible joy in Christ was virtually a standard and universal experi-ence among Christian believers."[5]

When churches overflow with love, joy, and all of the rest of the characteristics we've mentioned, there is another organic consequence: unbelievers are drawn to the community of faith and are converted. A Jesus person shares her faith, and another comes to Christ. He gives the gospel to two more, who tell four, who tell eight . . . this "good infection," as C. S. Lewis called it, was one of the hallmarks of the Jesus Movement.

One other note about revivals: Satan, the enemy of human souls, tries to corrupt and counterfeit them. Dr. Packer notes that in times of revival, Satan tries to use the false fire of fanaticism, the false zeal of errant teachers, and the false strategies of orthodox over-doers and divisive firebrands majoring in minors to discredit and demolish what God has been building up. Surely this was the case in the Jesus Movement. It spawned cults and prideful leaders who went off on their own paths. Critics nitpicked and missed blessings they might otherwise have enjoyed. Revivals are unorganized, messy, and fraught with risks for those who are not wearing the full armor of God.

Revivals also fade.

The spiritual awakening that rocked the "little country church" called Calvary Chapel is in the rearview mirror now. But the awakening was never about Calvary Chapel. Nor was it about Chuck Smith, or Lonnie Frisbee, or Greg Laurie, or any other person or church or denomination.

It was about Jesus moving by the power of His Holy Spirit in ordinary human lives.

We long for former days of revival not because we're nostalgic, trying to get the same experience back that we once had in the past. If we do that, our affections are sadly misplaced. No, we long for the Holy Spirit to fall upon us, our communities, and our nation in a fresh way so that God Himself would be glorified through the fruit and love of changed human lives.

What might it look like for Jesus to revive us again today? It needn't have a label, like a movement among a certain denomination or tradition, or among believers of a certain eschatological view. It needn't be confined to Christians from megachurches or minichurches, or to those who speak in tongues or those who don't. It needn't be the experience of just the hipsters or the oldsters, or just those who dunk or those who sprinkle. It will be where and when and with whom God chooses. It will be a beautiful mess—and let's just pray that it happens again. Soon.

It could be something we might call "mere revival."

During World War II, C. S. Lewis gave a series of radio lectures that became the slim volume *Mere Christianity*. This classic book has been seminal in the conversions of countless people, and has been on bestseller lists ever since it was released in the late 1940s. In it, Lewis likened Christianity to a big house with many rooms. The idea is that when we come to faith in Jesus Christ, we enter the house; we're in the grand, central hallway with other members of the body of Christ, or the church universal . . . all the human beings who will eventually all worship together in Heaven for eternity. It's a gloriously big hall.

But in this life individual Christians become part of local fellowships. The church particular: the *ekklesia*, visible gatherings of people who communally worship and grow in Christ. To use Lewis's analogy, once we're in God's house, we choose to go into one room or another. We find a particular group of believers to connect with, and we become an active and functioning part of a local church. We worship and grow with brothers and sisters who have commonly held traditions, liturgy, or doctrines.

But each human being in the house, under the same roof, comes in through the big hall and agrees to the essentials that followers of Jesus have held since He built His church in the first century. Lewis called these essentials—the hall—"mere" Christianity.

In the same sense, is this not a good time for believers in churches and fellowships all over America to pray earnestly for something big, something essential, something on which we all agree, something we might just call "mere revival"?

If He grants this yearning, extraordinary things will happen . . . but we do not pray for revival for its consequences, exciting as they are. We pray for revival today as a means for the extended glory of God, now and in eternity to come.

We pray that more and more people might come to know the One who made them, loves them, died to pay the just penalty for their sin, and rose from the dead so that those who believe in Him might one day also rise to give glory to Him around His throne, to revel in His love and enjoy Him forever.

EPILOGUE

Plunging In, All Over Again

You're back on Google Earth, zooming in on Southern California, Corona del Mar. There's that beach again, with its outcropping of cliffs that form a natural amphitheater near the mouth of the harbor. It really hasn't changed much since 1970, but now it's 2017.

As you get closer, you see that there is a huge crowd massing the area. People are perched all over the rocks, sitting on the sand, standing in the shallows of the rolling water. They have their arms around each other. They're singing, something about "You're a good, good Father" by some guy named Chris Tomlin, and "This is amazing grace," written by Phil Wickham, the son of two Jesus People who got married in the early '70s.

The sun is going down. The setting would look like a baptismal scene from the New Testament except for the iPhones that are everywhere, recording the event for Instagram and other social media. There is a row of pastors standing waist-deep in the Pacific, and new believers are wading out to them to be baptized. Some of the new Christians are teenagers, some are middle-aged, and almost all of them are weeping tears of joy, with huge, fresh smiles.

There is a teenaged boy. We'll call him Steven. He's seventeen. He's more quiet and reserved than the others, as if he still carries the burdens of his past dead ends of drug use, sexual promiscuity, and cynical despair. But he just gave his heart to Christ at an evangelistic event at Angel Stadium where some older guy was preaching the gospel, and Steven started going to his church and signed up to get baptized.

Steven wades out into the water. There's a pastor waiting for him. Wait, it's the old guy who preached at the crusade.

Greg Laurie smiles at Steven. "I asked for you," he says. "I asked to be able to baptize you, because I was seventeen when I received Christ and got baptized right here in this same spot. God has brought me through all kinds of things, good and bad, over the years, and He'll do the same for you."

"Thanks," says Steven. "I'm just done with the old stuff. I want to live for Jesus now."

They talk a bit more, then Greg carefully dunks the young man down in the cold water for a long moment. It's as if he's been buried.

Then Greg raises Steven up, and he bursts out of the sea, water streaming from his face and hair and shoulders. His heart is on his face, and he is weeping. Joy. Release. Freedom.

Greg is weeping too. Maybe God *will* bring revival for a new generation. And maybe, just maybe, he'll get to see another Jesus Revolution before he dies.

ACKNOWLEDGMENTS

Greg Laurie

It was around three years ago that one of the pastors on our staff, John Collins, told me it would be a good idea to meet a young filmmaker named Jon Erwin, who wanted to spend some time with me, as he had a lot of questions about a period of time I happened to live through.

Jon was in his early thirties at the time; he's made a number of outstanding films including *October Baby, Mom's Night Out, Woodlawn,* and *I Can Only Imagine.*

Woodlawn was the story of how the last great American revival, the Jesus Revolution, affected a school in Alabama, helping them to encounter God and, among other things, overcome their racism.

Jon was, in his words, "obsessed" with the Jesus Movement ever since he came across the *Time* magazine cover with the pop-art image of Christ and the words "The Jesus Revolution." He wanted to meet someone who was actually there to see it up close and personal.

I was.

As I saw Jon's interest in the smallest of details, and his thirst for seeing this kind of spiritual awakening for his generation, I got excited. When you're older, as I am now, you are sometimes reluctant to just tell stories from "the good old days."

But as I rehearsed what God had done fifty years ago, it reminded me that "Jesus Christ is the same yesterday and today and forever" (Heb. 13:8), and that God could indeed bring revival again.

The Jesus Revolution changed American and church history. An entire generation of young people who had believed the lies of the hippie utopia found what they were looking for, not in drugs, mysticism, or free sex, but in the pages of the Bible.

Out of this movement came many of the great leaders in the church today.

In these crazy times in which we are living, with mass shootings of innocent people, terrorism, the threat of nuclear war, and rampant racism, it seems to me that we are ripe for another spiritual awakening in America and around the world.

In short, we need another Jesus Revolution.

Out of my initial conversations with Jon Erwin came this book, and a feature film that will be shot in 2018.

I hope this book causes you to cry out to the Lord in prayer and say, "Lord, do it again!"

Prayerfully, He will.

"Will you not revive us again, that your people may rejoice in you?" (Ps. 85:6).

Greg Laurie
Irvine, California
November 2017

Ellen Vaughn

This book was written during an unprecedentedly difficult time of unexpected challenges and pain in my personal life. It was excellent to be able to delve into such strange and wonderful subject matter as the Jesus Revolution, and to have the luxury of writing—and reminding myself—of God's sovereignty and abiding love in times of chaos!

I am so grateful for the many faithful friends who prayed for me over recent months; the fact that this project was somehow completed in the midst of the crisis is a testimony to your kind support. Thank you, and much love, to: Patti Bryce, Carey Keefe, amazing heroes Mark and Norma Roessler, Mary Ann Bell, Babs and Rob Bickhart, Gloria Hawley, Gail Harwood, Norma Vaughn, Andi Brindley, Carole Schryber, Ellen Leitch, Janice Allen, Jamie Longo, Mariam Bell, Joanne Kemp and Friday Class, Jennifer Andrews, Shannon Davis, Lisa Catlett, Carmen Tamayo, Nicole Atkins, Laurie Hall Badwey, Paula Coe Corder, Michael and Diana Schick, Nancy Croker, Lisa Lampman, Sue Langlie, Rika Clark, Jane Daniel, Dale Sutherland, George and Connie Stewart, Bill and Miriam Shook, Arlita Winston, Valerie Elliot Shepard, Robert and Nancy DeMoss Wolgemuth, the board, staff, and friends of International Cooperating Ministries, McLean Bible Church, Mama Maggie Gobran and other dear friends in Egypt. Thank you, ye olde friends from Supper Club: Jim and Laura Warren, Scott and Sharon Hubbard, Tom and Tracey Pilsch, Susan Dawson, Rich and Lisa Hannibal, and Jeff and Nancy LeSourd. Thank you, Sunday night small group: Susie and Chris Knepper, Kelly and Erik Olafsson, Connie and Sam Shabshab, Kathleen and Armen Clark, Jen and Allen Herzberg, Amy and Jim Ellis, Kathy and Steve Matson. Thank you, CHEEKS—Connie again, Helen Link, Holly Leachman, Ellie Lofaro, and Kelly Stuckey. Thank you, HSM: Lou Sabatier, Jenna Mead, Sheila McGee, Sue Moye, Wendy Fotopolous, Janice Voth, Marcie Peck, Krisi Monsiviaz, and Joy Zorn. Everyone, your prayers carried us through many daunting challenges, and I am forever grateful.

Thank you, also, to the many friends and random people who told me their Jesus Movement stories. I wish that this had been the venue to include such tales, as they were all testimonies of God's great grace, sense of humor, and power at work in human lives.

Thank you to Jim Warren, Carole Schryber, Brad Ormonde, Leah Case, and Mary Ann Bell for reading and giving feedback on the manuscript. Thank you, John Schryber, for your insights about the 1967 Six-Day War, which were greatly consolidated in this book. Thank you, Chuck Fromm, for sharing your eloquent doctoral thesis about the Jesus Movement. Thank you to Robert, Andrew, and Erik Wolgemuth for your literary representation and for shepherding this project, and thank you to our friends at Baker Publishing Group for bringing this book to market.

Thank you to Greg and Cathe Laurie for your hospitality—and for feeding me—in many different settings, though I am secretly peeved that we did not have a chance to labor on this book somewhere near your church in Hawaii. Thanks for your insights, stories, and vulnerability, your odd and eccentric humor (Greg), and your lovely and compassionate spirit (Cathe). You guys have been dear friends for a long time, and I am so grateful for you and for your faithful hearts for Jesus. Thank you so much to all the Harvest staff who answered questions, made interviews possible, and eased my way into various venues.

Thank you to Emily, Haley, and Walker for your solidarity and support, as always. And thank you, Lee Vaughn, for your faithful encouragement and for putting up with me for multiple decades! You are such a patient, wonderful, and godly man.

Most of all, I am overwhelmed and grateful to God for the way He so graciously rescues us, right in the midst of our mess. That's the story of the Jesus Revolution, and I hope that He might somehow use this humble book to refresh readers with the reality of His love and power—for His glory—in these desperate times.

Ellen Vaughn
Reston, Virginia
Thanksgiving 2017

NOTES

Chapter 1 What Was It and Why Does It Matter?

1. Drew Dyck, "Millennials Don't Need a Hipper Pastor, They Need a Bigger God," *Church Leaders*, August 17, 2014, https://churchleaders .com/pastors/pastor-articles/175857-drew-dyck-millennials-need-a-bigger -god-not-a-hipper-pastor.html.

2. If you want a scholarly or more comprehensive overview of the whole Jesus Movement across the United States, we recommend *God's Forever Family* by Larry Eskridge (New York: Oxford University Press, 2013).

Chapter 2 A Black-and-White Decade

1. In 1890, 4 percent of the country's married women were in the work-force; in 1940 there were only 15 percent; but by April 1956, 30 percent of married women held jobs. In 1940, only 7 percent of mothers with children under five years old held jobs; by 1955 the number had jumped to 18.2 percent. See Daniel Bell, "The Great Back-to-Work Movement (*Fortune*, 1956)," *Fortune*, September 16, 2012, http://fortune.com/2012 /09/16/the-great-back-to-work-movement-fortune-1956/.

2. See Stanley Rothman, *The End of the Experiment: The Rise of Cultural Elites and the Decline of America's Civic Culture* (Piscataway, NJ: Transaction Publishers, 2015).

3. Robert Ellwood, *The Fifties Spiritual Marketplace: American Religion in a Decade of Conflict* (New Brunswick, NJ: Rutgers University Press, 1997), 5.

Chapter 3 The Wonderful World of Color

1. "Radio: Big As All Outdoors," *Time*, October 17, 1955.

2. Mikal Gilmore, "Beatles' Acid Test: How LSD Opened the Door to 'Revolver,'" *Rolling Stone*, August 25, 2016, http://www.rollingstone

.com/music/news/beatles-revolver-how-lsd-opened-the-door-to-a-mas
terpiece-w436062.

3. Gilmore, "Beatles' Acid Test."

Chapter 4 The Pastor Who Downscaled

1. From Charles E. Fromm, "Textual Communities and New Song in
the Multimedia Age: The Routinization of Charisma in the Jesus Movement" (PhD diss., Fuller Theological Seminary, February 2006).

2. Luke 4:18–19.

3. See Joel 2:28–29 and Acts 2:17.

4. Jordan Runtagh, "When John Lennon's 'More Popular Than Jesus'
Controversy Turned Ugly," *Rolling Stone*, July 29, 2016, http://www
.rollingstone.com/music/features/when-john-lennons-jesus-controversy
-turned-ugly-w431153.

5. Runtagh, "John Lennon's 'More Popular Than Jesus' Controversy."

6. John T. Elson, "Is God Dead?" *Time*, April 8, 1966.

7. Per Faxneld and Jesper Aagaard Petersen, eds., *The Devil's Party:
Satanism in Modernity* (New York: Oxford University Press, 2013), 79–82.

Chapter 5 The Be-In, the Summer of Love, and a Nudist Vegetarian Hippie

1. Sheila Weller, "Suddenly That Summer," *Vanity Fair*, July 2012,
http://www.vanityfair.com/culture/2012/07/lsd-drugs-summer-of-love
-sixties.

2. "500 Greatest Albums of All Time," *Rolling Stone*, May 31, 2012,
http://www.rollingstone.com/music/lists/500-greatest-albums-of-all-time
-20120531/the-beatles-sgt-peppers-lonely-hearts-club-band-20120531.

3. "500 Greatest Albums of All Time."

Chapter 6 Miracle in the Middle East

1. Committee for Accuracy in Middle East Reporting in America
(CAMERA), "Precursors to War: Arab Threats Against Israel," *The Six-
Day War*, accessed January 3, 2018, http://www.sixdaywar.org/content
/threats.asp.

2. Ahmed Shukairy, as quoted in "6 Days War: Crucial Quotes," accessed January 3, 2018, http://www.sixdaywar.co.uk/crucial_quotes.htm.

3. See Daniel 8, which records Daniel's complicated vision of about
539 BC and its equally mysterious interpretation. In the vision, Daniel
saw himself in the Persian capital of Susa, in modern-day Iran, near the
border with Iraq:

I, Daniel, had a vision. . . . I looked up, and there before me was a ram with two horns, standing beside the canal, and the horns were long. . . . Suddenly a goat with a prominent horn between its eyes came from the west, crossing the whole earth without touching the ground. It came toward the two-horned ram . . . and charged at it in great rage. I saw it attack the ram furiously, striking the ram and shattering its two horns. The ram was powerless to stand against it; the goat knocked it to the ground and trampled on it, and none could rescue the ram from its power. (vv. 1–7)

This part of Daniel's strange prophecy was fulfilled when Alexander the Great, with an army of 35,000 Greeks and Macedonians, crossed northwestern Turkey into Asia Minor in 334 BC and soundly defeated the vast and powerful Persian Empire.

Chapter 7 1968: And the Wind Began to Howl

1. "George Harrison," Wikipedia, last modified August 5, 2017, https://en.wikiquote.org/wiki/George_Harrison.

2. Ben Fong-Torres, "Harrison Had Love-Haight Relationship with S.F.," *SFGate*, December 2, 2001, http://www.sfgate.com/entertainment/radiowaves/article/Harrison-had-love-Haight-relationship-with-S-F-2847011.php.

3. Lonnie Frisbee with Roger Sachs, *Not by Might Nor by Power: The Jesus Revolution*, 2nd ed. (Santa Maria, CA: Freedom Publications, 2012), 50.

4. For a far more comprehensive overview of the Jesus Movement in general across the United States, and of the Wises' involvement in particular, see Larry Eskridge, *God's Forever Family* (New York: Oxford University Press, 2013).

5. Associated Press, "Tapes: Johnson Was Leery on Vietnam," *Washington Post*, November 2, 2001, http://www.washingtonpost.com/wp-srv/aponline/20011102/aponline185308_000.htm.

6. Martin Luther King Jr., "I Have a Dream," speech, August 28, 1963, Washington, DC, https://www.archives.gov/files/press/exhibits/dream-speech.pdf.

7. Martin Luther King Jr., "I've Been to the Mountaintop," speech delivered April 3, 1968, Mason Temple (Church of God in Christ Headquarters), Memphis, Tennessee; *American Rhetoric*, accessed January 29, 2018, http://www.americanrhetoric.com/speeches/mlkivebeentothemountaintop.htm.

8. "Robert F. Kennedy's Speech on the Assassination of Martin Luther King Jr.," Wikipedia, last modified December 19, 2017, https://en.wiki

pedia.org/wiki/Robert_F._Kennedy%27s_speech_on_the_assassination _of_Martin_Luther_King_Jr.

9. "Robert F. Kennedy Speeches," John F. Kennedy Presidential Library and Museum, accessed January 3, 2018, https://www.jfklibrary.org/Re search/Research-Aids/Ready-Reference/RFK-Speeches/Statement-on-the -Assassination-of-Martin-Luther-King.aspx.

10. Steve Lopez, "The Busboy Who Cradled a Dying RFK Has Finally Stepped Out of the Past," *Los Angeles Times*, August 29, 2015, http://www .latimes.com/local/california/la-me-0830-lopez-romero-20150829-column .html.

Chapter 8 When Nitro Met Glycerin

1. This conversation, and similar accounts from the early days of Chuck and Lonnie's ministry, is adapted from Chuck Smith with Hugh Steven, *The Reproducers: New Life for Thousands* (Glendale, CA: Regal Books, 1972).

2. See Acts 2:42.

3. 1 John 4:7–11.

Chapter 10 Magnificent Desolation

1. John F. Kennedy, "Excerpt from the 'Special Message to the Congress on Urgent National Needs,'" speech delivered before a joint session of Congress May 25, 1961, *NASA History*, May 24, 2004, https://www.nasa .gov/vision/space/features/jfk_speech_text.html; "John F. Kennedy Moon Speech—Rice Stadium," speech delivered September 12, 1962, NASA, accessed January 30, 2018, https://er.jsc.nasa.gov/seh/ricetalk.htm.

2. Adrienne Lafrance, "Buzz Aldrin on the Moon: 'More Desolate Than Any Place on Earth,'" *The Atlantic*, July 8, 2014, https://www .theatlantic.com/technology/archive/2014/07/buzz-aldrin-on-the-moon -more-desolate-than-any-place-on-earth/374123/.

3. "Did Woodstock Change America?" *Think Tank with Ben Wattenberg*, PBS, August 5, 1994, http://www.pbs.org/thinktank/transcript 119.html.

4. "Did Woodstock Change America?"

5. "Did Woodstock Change America?"

6. Richard Brody, "What Died at Altamont," *New Yorker*, March 11, 2015, https://www.newyorker.com/culture/richard-brody/what -died-at-altamont.

7. David Browne, "Grace Slick's Festival Memories: Fearing Orgies and Getting Lit," *Rolling Stone*, May 23, 2014, http://www.rollingstone .com/music/news/grace-slicks-festival-memories-fearing-orgies-and -getting-lit-20140523.

8. "Statement on the Historical and Cultural Significance of the 1969 Woodstock Festival Site," Woodstock Preservation Archives, September 25, 2001, http://www.woodstockpreservation.org/SignificanceStatement.htm (emphasis added).

Chapter 11 The Long and Winding Road

1. See Linda Goodman, *Sun Signs* (New York: Taplinger Publishing Co., 1968).

Chapter 12 The Adult in the Room

1. Chuck Smith, *The History of Calvary Chapel* (pamphlet), 26, https://s3.amazonaws.com/storage.nm-storage.com/calvaryarlington/downloads/history_cc.pdf.

2. Smith, *History of Calvary Chapel*, 28.

Chapter 13 Jesus Music

1. Fromm, "Textual Communities," 297.

Chapter 14 Life as Usual, inside the Revolution

1. See Luke 8:4–15.

2. C. S. Lewis, *The Screwtape Letters*, rev. ed. (New York: Macmillan, 1982), 13–14.

3. L. E. Romaine, Facebook, February 17, 2017, https://www.facebook.com/leromaine/.

4. John 4:14.

5. As quoted in Smith, *The Reproducers*, 89.

Chapter 15 No Bare Feet Allowed!

1. Adapted from Smith, *History of Calvary Chapel*, 29–30.

2. Chuck Girard and Fred Field, "Little Country Church" © 1971 by Dunamis Music.

Chapter 17 Love Story

1. "The Alternative Jesus: Psychedelic Christ," *Time*, June 21, 1971.

2. American folk hymn.

Chapter 18 Billy Graham's Good Vibrations

1. Billy Graham's quotes in this chapter are all drawn from Billy Graham, *The Jesus Generation* (London: Hodder & Stoughton, 1971).

2. Edward B. Fiske, "A 'Religious Woodstock' Draws 75,000," *New York Times*, June 16, 1972, http://www.nytimes.com/1972/06/16/archives /a-religious-woodstock-draws-75000-a-religious-woodstock-explo-72 .html.

3. "What Really Happened at Explo '72," *Cru*, October 15, 2015, htt ps://www.cru.org/about/what-we-do/what-really-happened-at-explo -72.html.

Chapter 19 The Church of Stone

1. Psalm 118:5.

Chapter 20 If You Can Explain It, Then God Didn't Do It

1. See, for example, Warren W. Wiersbe, *He Walks with Me: Enjoying the Abiding Presence of God* (Colorado Springs: David C. Cook, 2016).

Chapter 21 Hippie Preachers

1. "About Don," Calvary Way Ministries, https://calvaryway.com /ministries/calvary-way/.

2. "Steve Mays—Memorial for My Pastor," *Walking the Berean Road* (blog), October 22, 2014, https://walkingthebereanroad.com/2014/10/22 /pastor-steve-mays/.

Chapter 22 Malaise and the Me Decade

1. I. F. Stone, "Nixon's War Gamble and Why It Won't Work," *New York Review of Books*, June 1, 1972, http://www.nybooks.com/articles /1972/06/01/iif-stone-reportsi-nixons-war-gamble-and-why-it-wo/.

2. Quoted in Ben Alpers, "Whatever Happened to the 'Me Decade'?" *U.S. Intellectual History* (blog), April 4, 2015, https://s-usih.org/2015/04 /whatever-happened-to-the-me-decade/.

3. Jimmy Carter, "Address to the Nation on Energy and National Goals: 'The Malaise Speech,'" July 15, 1979, http://www.presidency.ucsb .edu/ws/?pid=32596.

4. Carter, "The Malaise Speech."

Chapter 23 Tea or Revolution?

1. Frisbee, *Not by Might*, 195.

2. Matt Coker, "Ears on Their Heads, but They Don't Hear," *OC Weekly*, April 14, 2005, http://www.ocweekly.com/film/ears-on-their -heads-but-they-dont-hear-6399415.

3. Frisbee, *Not by Might*, 192–93.

4. Quoted in Vicky Dillen, "What Happened in Africa?" *Seek God*, accessed January 3, 2018, http://www.seekgod.ca/bantu.htm.

Chapter 25 Muscle Memory

1. Job 1:21.

2. From C. S. Lewis, *Surprised by Joy*, as quoted in Art Lindsley, "C. S. Lewis: His Life and Works," C. S. Lewis Institute, http://www.cslewisin stitute.org/node/28.

3. "A Lifetime of Impact," Greg Laurie interview with Pastor Chuck Smith, https://vimeo.com/34646573.

4. "A Lifetime of Impact."

5. "A Lifetime of Impact."

Chapter 26 Desperate Enough?

1. Elmer Towns and Douglas Porter, *The Ten Greatest Revivals Ever* (Ann Arbor, MI: Servant Publications, 2000), 58.

2. Towns and Porter, *Ten Greatest Revivals*, 58.

3. Revelation 3:15–18.

4. Revelation 3:19–20.

5. Please check out this rich essay by J. I. Packer, "The Glory of God and the Reviving of Religion," delivered at the Desiring God 2003 National Conference on October 11, 2003, https://www.desiringgod.org/messages /the-glory-of-god-and-the-reviving-of-religion (emphasis added).

Chapter 27 Cultural Christianity Is Dead: Rest in Peace

1. *American Experience—Summer of Love*, directed by Vicente Franco (Arlington, VA: PBS, 2007), DVD. Transcript available at http://www.pbs .org/wgbh/ amex/love/filmmore/pt.html. Emphasis added.

Chapter 28 Mere Revival

1. John Wagner and Scott Clement, "'It's Just Messed Up': Most Think Political Divisions as Bad as Vietnam Era, New Poll Shows," *Washington Post*, October 28, 2017, https://www.washingtonpost.com/graphics/2017 /national/democracy-poll/?utm_term=.306488d9ee96.

2. Packer, "Glory of God."

3. Acts 3:19.

4. Jonathan Edwards, *A Faithful Narrative of the Surprising Works of God* (repr. Revival Press, 2016), 16.

5. Packer, "Glory of God."

Greg Laurie is the senior pastor of Harvest Christian Fellowship with campuses in California and Hawaii. He began his pastoral ministry at the age of nineteen by leading a Bible study of thirty people. Since then, God has transformed that small group into a church of some fifteen thousand people. Today, Harvest is one of the largest churches in America.

In 1990, Greg Laurie began holding large-scale public evangelistic events called Harvest Crusades. Since that time, in-person attendance and live webcast views for these events have totaled more than 8.7 million, with 506,644 people deciding to make a profession of faith in Jesus Christ. Laurie was also the speaker at Harvest America in Arlington, Texas, in 2016; with an attendance of 350,000 it was deemed the largest live one-day evangelistic event in US history.

Along with his work at Harvest Ministries, Greg Laurie served as the 2013 Honorary Chairman of the National Day of Prayer, and also serves on the board of directors of the Billy Graham Evangelistic Association. He holds honorary doctorates from Biola University and Azusa Pacific University.

Greg Laurie has a daily nationally syndicated radio program, *A New Beginning*, which is broadcast on more than one thousand radio outlets around the world, as well as a weekly television program.

Greg Laurie has authored over seventy books, including *Steve McQueen: The Salvation of an American Icon*, *Live Love Fight*, *Tell Someone*, *Greatest Stories Ever Told*, *Hope for Hurting Hearts*, and his autobiography, *Lost Boy*. The accompanying documentary film, *Lost Boy: The Next Chapter*, has won eight awards at international film festivals. His 2013 film *Hope for Hurting Hearts* features his story of trusting God through tragedy. A new documentary film, *Steve McQueen: American Icon*, is now out on DVD.

Greg has been married to Cathe Laurie for forty-three years and they have two sons, Christopher and Jonathan. Christopher went to be with the Lord in 2008. Greg and Cathe also have five grandchildren.

Ellen Vaughn is a *New York Times* bestselling author who has written or co-written twenty-three books. Former vice president of executive communications for Prison Fellowship, she collaborated with the late Chuck Colson on a number of his seminal works. She speaks at conferences and retreats, often travels to interview Christians in hostile parts of the world, and serves as a senior fellow for the 21st Century Wilberforce Initiative and on the board of directors for International Cooperating Ministries. With degrees from Georgetown University and the University of Richmond, Ellen is mom to two grown daughters and a son, and lives in her northern Virginia empty nest with her husband, Lee, a regional pastor at McLean Bible Church, and two enthusiastic but clueless dogs.

HARVEST MINISTRIES
ONLINE TRAINING COURSES

TELL SOMEONE
Get equipped to confidently share your faith in Christ with boldness and tact. This free online course will help you use your personal testimony to build a bridge and bring the Good News of Jesus to those around you.

WHAT EVERY GROWING CHRISTIAN NEEDS TO KNOW
As believers, it is important that we grow in our relationship with Jesus Christ. We all should have a desire to be mature, growing Christians. There are key disciplines that we must follow to effectively grow, and Harvest wants to help you understand and establish those habits.

NEW BELIEVERS ONLINE COURSE
It's important to get off on the right foot in our walk with Christ. And to do that, we must develop good spiritual habits, like reading God's Word and praying daily, attending church regularly, and sharing our faith. In this course, Pastor Jonathan Laurie takes us through the four steps that every new believer needs to take in order to become a strong, mature follower of Jesus.

HAPPINESS ONLINE COURSE
People chase after many things trying to find happiness, things like fame, wealth, and pleasure. But in the end, those things only leave a feeling of emptiness and misery. According to Scripture, the only place to find true happiness is in a relationship with God. In this course, Pastor Greg shows us how to find that true happiness by following Jesus and loving others.

GET STARTED AT
COURSES.HARVEST.ORG

God is in the business of transforming His followers into world changers,
AND THAT INCLUDES YOU!

 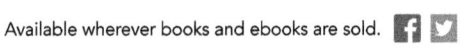

Connect with

BakerBooks

Relevant. Intelligent. Engaging.

Sign up for announcements about new and upcoming titles at

BakerBooks.com/SignUp

@ReadBakerBooks